Badger Book Series

Would Jesus Do Time?

Pain Bleeds a Heroine

Medicaria (available 5-29-26)

The Andrew Jackson Defense (available 6-28-26)

Master of Statecraft (available 7-11-26)

A Private Prison Web (available 8-27-26)

Eclipse City (available 10-24-26)

Dates subject to change

Pain Bleeds a Heroine

ISBN 979-8-234-04732-8 (paperback)

Pain Bleeds a Heroine

by

J. L. Chaffin

For Vicki,

who waved a hand like a goddess

and made it all happen.

Thank you, my love.

Pain Bleeds a Heroine

EXT. ATLANTIC OCEAN – DAY

Out on the vastness of the Atlantic Ocean is a single ship: the Haverford. It's headed for a storm, maybe ten miles away. A beam of sunlight shines on the top of ALICE PAUL's (25) dark, brown hair.

She glances up at it, but the fiery ray is smothered out by foreboding clouds. She refocuses on the storm ahead. Her clothes are fashionable, upscale. Her skin is pallid, and she's very skinny. But her eyes are ablaze with strength and determination.

Lightening cracks and is reflected in her eyes.

EXT. PHILADELPHIA, PENNSYLVANIA - DAY

SUPER: January 20, 1910

Alice walks down a Philadelphia gangplank and onto dry ground. People spot her and try unsuccessfully to lower their voices to talk about her so she can't hear.

PASSERBY
Oh my, that's Alice Paul, is it not?

MALE CIVILIAN
She's going to start trouble over *here* now.

OBSERVER
She needs to go back over the Atlantic and stay there.

Alice ignores them. She has eyes only for her mother TACIE PAUL (50s) and her 15-year-old sister PARRY. Her mother's hand flies to her mouth upon seeing Alice's fragile state. The family hugs.

ALICE
Hello, Mother. How are thee?

Note: Alice, her mother, and sister use thees and thys — the Quaker dialect — when speaking to each other.

                          MRS. PAUL
Well. Very well, Alice. But look at thee! We must get some food into thy body.

Also waiting for Alice are REPORTERS and PHOTOGRAPHERS. The photographers' cameras shutter as she greets her mother and sister. One JOURNALIST can't help but to interrupt the family reunion.

                          JOURNALIST
Miss Paul, will you take part in the movement here in America?

                            ALICE
I didn't know there was a movement here, but if the opportunity arises, I shall certainly do what I can.

                          REPORTER
There are many well-to-do American women working for suffrage.

                            ALICE
The suffrage movement here will not get far so long as its patronage is limited to society women. It must be a universal movement, in which *all* women must join and work for the common cause.

Mrs. Paul grabs Alice's hand, as does Parry, and they lead her toward their carriage. Reporters continue to badger her.

                          JOURNALIST
Do you believe militancy will be as useful in America as it is in England?

                            ALICE
Militancy will not serve well in the United States. We are much freer over here, so I do not foresee us having to go through such extremes to win the vote. But if it becomes necessary to fight to win, I believe in fighting.

REPORTER
We know you do.

Alice and her family step into the carriage and ride off.

EXT. MRS. PAUL'S HOUSE - DAY

Sat in the middle of a farm is the Paul residence. Sheep graze on the lawn. The carriage pulls up to it. Alice, Mrs. Paul, and Parry hurry out.

ALICE
Everything looks the same. The only thing missing...

PARRY
Is Father.

Mrs. Paul throws her arms over them and rubs their shoulders.

MRS. PAUL
Don't fret. Thy brother and sister will be with us shortly. Then the place won't appear so empty. Now, let thy mother feed thee.

She escorts her two daughters into the house.

MRS. PAUL (CONT'D)
Thee knows where thy father's burial site is, so thee can always pay him a visit.

INT. MRS. PAUL'S HOUSE - CONTINUOUS

Parry grabs a stack of mail as soon as they enter the house.

PARRY
Look at all this mail that came for thee during the past fortnight. Mother thinks it's the many women's suffrage organizations seeking to recruit thee.

Parry hands Alice all of her mail, which is secured in strings and seems to be around a couple dozen letters.

MRS. PAUL
I imagine many of them are fan letters, as well. I also saved all the newspaper articles about thee, too.

Mrs. Paul goes into the closet to grab the newspapers, but it appears she's handling more than mere news. More like bad memories, heartbreak, deadly paraphernalia for good mental health.
ALICE
This is more than I received in England.

PARRY
There's more on thy bed from over the summer and fall when thee became a celebrity.

Mrs. Paul quickly drops the newspapers into Alice's hands as if they were a disease she couldn't wait to be rid of. She escapes into the kitchen to prepare dinner. Alice gives a questioning look to her mother before reading a headline from the newspaper on top of the pile.
ALICE
"AMERICAN WOMAN AND FIFTY THOUSAND OTHER WOMEN STORM PARLIAMENT."
(chuckles)
Makes me sound like I was the leader.
(reads another headline)
"ALICE PAUL ON HUNGER STRIKE IN LONDON PRISON."

Alice winces after reading this out loud in front of her mother. She reads the other headlines silently: "MISS ALICE PAUL IS THE FIRST SUFFRAGETTE JAILED IN SCOTLAND" and "OUR ALICE PAUL BREAKS WINDOW AT GUILDHALL TO DEMAND VOTES FOR WOMEN."

                              MRS. PAUL
I don't want thee using the militancy methods being
practiced in England.

                                ALICE
Mother, I — —

Mrs. Paul slams a cupboard and rounds on Alice.

                              MRS. PAUL

— — Thee almost died!

Her hand shoots to her throat, shocked by her own outburst. She
turns back around to hide her shame at her lack of self-control.
She returns to preparing dinner. Alice is equally as shocked, but
gathers herself quickly.
                                ALICE
                              (softly)
I will no longer use the word "militancy" when describing
my methods, because it connotes thoughts of violence, and
I've never hurt anyone. Thee knows this.

Mrs. Paul faces Alice, very composed now.

                              MRS. PAUL
And thee knows what I am referring to. I don't want thee
to commit crimes, to go to jail, or to go on hunger strikes.
I want thee to return to school.

Alice smiles and hugs her mother.

                                ALICE
                             (whispers)
That is exactly what I plan to do, Mother.

Mrs. Paul separates from Alice and looks her squarely in the eyes.

MRS. PAUL
Thee also shouldn't overwork thyself. People quite literally die from over-exertion, Alice, and I know how singularly focused thee can become on a task, forgetting to eat, hydrate, and sleep.

Alice's eyes penetrate hers just as deeply.

ALICE
I will be sure to take care of myself, Mother.

Mrs. Paul's expression leads us to believe she knows her daughter better than Alice knows herself. She steps away from her, leaving Alice staring after Mrs. Paul indignantly.

INT. MRS. PAUL'S HOUSE - ALICE'S ROOM - NIGHT

Alice is moaning, tossing and turning. She appears to be having a nightmare.
ALICE
(moaning/dreaming)
No... No, please...

DREAM/FLASHBACK - ALICE IN PRISON

Several men attired in prison guard uniforms are brutally kicking a naked Alice Paul in her cell. It's merciless.

They're kicking her with everything they've got. After rendering her unconscious, they carry her out of the cell.

BACK TO SCENE

Alice awakes by sitting up suddenly. She stares at nothing until she realizes where she is. She begins trembling, then crying. She suppresses a scream by covering her mouth with a blanket.

INT. MRS. PAUL'S HOUSE - DAY

Mrs. Paul is making her way to Alice's room. She knocks before opening the door. Alice is reading her mail while lying on her bed when her mom steps in.

> ALICE
>
> Mother, I've inspired all these women to fight for the ballot. Thee should hear their stories. One of them was beaten by her husband, took her complaint to the district attorney of her city, and was denied justice. She wanted to vote the attorney out of office but couldn't, obviously.

> MRS. PAUL
>
> Honey — —

> ALICE
>
> — — Wait. There's one who has a similar story to mine. She was beaten by police when she was protesting, tried to file criminal charges against the officer, and the police commissioner suppressed it. She wanted to vote a more honest man into that position and also couldn't. We NEED the right to vote, Mother.

> MRS. PAUL
>
> Honey, it's great that thee is inspiring people, but thee has visitors.

Alice is off the bed and on her feet before Mrs. Paul finishes pronouncing the last syllable in "visitors."

> MRS. PAUL (CONT'D)
>
> They're helping themselves to some tea.

INT. MRS. PAUL'S HOUSE - LIVING ROOM - DAY

Two women stand on seeing Alice enter the room. One is

HARRIOT STANTON BLATCH (50s) and the other is INEZ MILHOLLAND (late 20s). Three glasses of tea sit on a coffee table in front of them. Harriet reaches her hand out.

HARRIOT
Hello, Alice, my name is Harriot Blatch.

They shake hands. Alice codeswitches for them and drops the thees and thys, but she also realizes she's heard of her.

ALICE
You're the... Oh, thank you so much for pressuring British officials about my release from jail. Please. Come here.

She hugs Harriot.
HARRIOT
It's my pleasure making men squirm.

They laugh and part. Inez (considered the most beautiful suffragist of the time) reaches out her hand and shakes Alice's.

INEZ
And I'm Inez Milholland. It's so nice to meet you.

Alice gestures at a couch for them to sit on.

ALICE
It's a pleasure to meet you. Shall we have a seat?

They sit. Alice sits in a chair across from them.

HARRIOT
Thank you. Inez and I are from New York. I'm sure you've had others approach you asking for you to join their suffrage groups, but — —

ALICE
— — Oh, I haven't had anybody approach me. I've received many letters and offers to join various organizations, but you two are the first to pay me a visit.

Harriot and Inez eye each other and smile.

                         HARRIOT
          Told you it was wise to leave when we did.

They try unsuccessfully to rein in their looks of triumph as their
eyes find Alice's again.

                          ALICE
          Speaking of letters, I've received a lot from women telling
          me their reason why they need the right to vote. If you
          don't mind sharing, I'd like to hear yours.

                          INEZ
          For me, I had an office job and many men thought they
          could put their hands on me inappropriately. They'd
          always say I was asking for it with how "beautiful" I was.
                    (shakes head)
          Well, there was a similar scandal going on with a
          congressman who was coming up for re-election, and he
          was exactly like the men I worked with. Of course, he was
          voted back in office, but I wished I could've voted against
          him.

Harriot's lips purse.

                         HARRIOT
          The husband of my cousin raped her. We went to the
          police, attorneys, and even judges looking for justice. They
          all acted like it was a husband's right. I knew then things
          had to change, and it started with women having power.

Alice's countenance is one of anger, but her eyes are very shiny
with liquid.

                          ALICE
          This is what we're fighting for. Thank you both.

They nod. There's a moment of silence.

                          INEZ
          Back to the matter at hand.

                        HARRIOT
          We're not here to ask you to join the Equality League of
          Self Supporting Women — —

                          INEZ
          — — Technically I'm connected to several suffrage
          organizations.
                        HARRIOT
          She has no allegiance to anybody.

                          INEZ
          My allegiance is to *ALL* women.

Inez winks at Alice. Harriot sighs and continues.

                        HARRIOT
          I would love for you to join my organization, but we're here
          to invite you to speak in New York and see for yourself
          what the Equality League of Self-Supporting Women has
          to offer *you*.
                         ALICE
          I want to help in any way I can, but I don't want to be the
          face of any group. That's not the way I desire to lead.

                          INEZ
          What vision do you have for yourself?

                         ALICE
          First, I plan on going back to school to obtain my doctorate
          in political science.

The two women grin and nod their heads.

                        HARRIOT
          Hmm. Soon we'll be calling you Doctor Paul, eh?

ALICE
No, Miss Paul would be fine by me. Ultimately, I would like to observe what efforts are being utilized here and decide on my own course of action.

Both women nod again, very impressed with this woman.

INEZ
So, would you be willing to speak in New York next week?

HARRIOT
We will pay for your train, accommodations, and everything else you will need.

ALICE
That's very kind of you. I happily agree to be of service.

Mrs. Paul enters the room.

MRS. PAUL
Pardon me. Alice, more visitors have arrived for thee. I shall fix more tea.

Inez and Harriot make questioning looks at each other. Alice responds to their curious faces as she stands and pulls back a curtain to see out a window.

ALICE
We're Quakers, so we use thees and thys when speaking to each other.

Alice watches carriages arrive one after the other. Women march on the house, toward Alice, toward freedom. Alice closes her mouth and tilts her head up.

ALICE (CONT'D)
Inez... What's the name of this congressman?

INT. U.S CAPITOL - DAY

                    GRETA
Congressman Banks!

GRETA GRAHAM (20s) rushes up to CONGRESSMAN BANKS (50s), a smooth-looking man with slick-backed hair and a politician's smile.

                    BANKS
What can I do for you, ma'am?

                    GRETA
Hi, my name is Greta Graham. I'm straight out of Montana State University. I've passed the Bar and have been writing your office in Montana for months in hopes of obtaining an internship.

Congressman Banks is shocked at first that this *WOMAN* wants an internship. He can't help but laugh.

                    BANKS
Listen, this job isn't as easy as you might think, little lady.

                    GRETA
I truly want to be of service to the people of Montana. I want to *help*, Mr. Banks. Please. I've never wanted anything more in my life.

Congressman Bank's predatory eyes snap to attention at this statement.

                    GRETA (CONT'D)
Your secretary told me the best time to speak with you was clear across the country. Here in our nation's capital. Do you think I would travel all the way to Washington D.C. if I weren't ready to work terribly hard for you?

A wolfish grin comes on Banks.

BANKS
Perhaps we could take a train back together and I could
interview you then.

Greta smiles, but there's a discomfort in it due to Banks's slimy
grin and slithery tone.

INT. NEW YORK AUDITORIUM - DAY

Alice stands off to the side of a stage as Harriot speaks to a
massive audience. Inez grabs Alice's hand and squeezes it.

INEZ
You're going to be great. I know it.

Inez releases her hand.

ALICE
I better. I've done a lot of this overseas, but...
(rubs hands)
This is very important. It's bigger than me, bigger than us.
It's truly for the world.

HARRIOT
And now let me introduce to you all one of the most
impressive women I have ever met: Miss Alice Paul!

Harriot applauds along with the audience as Alice takes the stage.
Alice waits for the clapping to turn to silence.

ALICE
Thank you, Miss Blatch... I know there are a lot of
questions surrounding me and the "militancy" efforts I
was supposedly involved with in England and Scotland,
and I'd like to quash these before diving into the real issues
at hand. First off, let me say *no one* has ever been injured
in the suffrage cause, except the suffragettes.

EXT. PHILADELPHIA EVENT - DAY

Alice is speaking in front of hundreds of people.

ALICE

The price suffragettes pay for their freedom is terribly dear, but they are convinced that only the methods of war and practical politics will ever win their cause. Some women have become permanently hurt and broken in health, but for that, they care nothing.

INT. OHIO CONVENTION - DAY

Alice speaks in front of another massive audience.

ALICE

The giving of the ballot would be but the public recognition of the change which social forces have brought about. After seeing a woman enter the political realm, it only makes sense for women to demand the ballot for themselves. It was but a natural step.

INT. NAWSA CONVENTION - DAY

Alice is speaking to the biggest crowd yet.

ALICE

We are all so wretchedly well-to-do, we dread anything disturbing. Even an idea. You all should not judge the Pankhursts and their fight in England based on the American press. It's rife with distortion. Women of *all* classes are fighting for the ballot. They are in deadly earnest. And for those of you still in doubt, I ask you to remember this: "Resistance to tyranny is obedience to God."

The audience cheers and applauds. When the cheers begin to die down, one ANGRY MAN stands and shouts over the noise at her.

                         ANGRY MAN
Do you think it a Christian act to break a window? Do you believe God would approve of that?

A SUFFRAGETTE'S HUSBAND also in the crowd shouts him down.

                    SUFFRAGETTE'S HUSBAND
Sit down!

ALICE'S VISION - ACTIVISM IN ENGLAND

Alice has a bunch of angry men shouting at her as she speaks. A sign behind her reads, "WOMEN NEED TO VOTE." One MISOGYNIST points at her.

                         MISOGYNIST
Go sit down somewhere.

The angry men then begin throwing rocks at her.

BACK TO SCENE

Alice ducks one "rock" only she can see. Then another. She blinks and realizes where she is. She gets a hold of herself and reality. She straightens her dress.

                           ALICE
No, I'll answer him. In England, many politicians refused to listen or even sit with women to hear our cry for help, so, yes, I did break a window and voice my view to a politician. But, sir, I find no sanctity in a pane of glass...
In fact, I had broken forty-eight, not just the one you heard of.

                    SUFFRAGETTE'S HUSBAND
Hear hear!

Applause. Alice waves at them all and exits the stage. Many people come up to her and congratulate her for a "fine speech." She is very gracious with her time and attention.

A gray-haired woman in her fifties named DORA LEWIS approaches Alice.

                            DORA
What a beautiful speech and *great* comeback for that ignorant boob.

Alice grins.

                            ALICE
Thank you.

                            DORA
Forgive me for prying, but I saw you on stage...
                    (Alice's face reddens)
Try taking deep calming breaths whenever your past struggles come upon you. It helped my father after the Civil War.

Alice nods, but she can hardly look her in the eyes. Dora notices her embarrassment and changes the subject.

                    DORA (CONT'D)
How does it feel to have everybody want you to speak for them and their groups? I can't imagine. They're all saying, "If only we can secure Alice Paul for our convention, it'll be a success." You are an amazing speaker, so now I can see why.
                    (extends her hand)
Name's Dora, by the way. Dora Lewis.

Alice shakes her hand.
                            ALICE
It's a pleasure to meet you.

                    DORA
The pleasure is mine.

They part and grin at each other.

                 DORA (CONT'D)
I'm the chair of local arrangements for the National
American Women Suffrage Association.

                    ALICE
The biggest organization for woman's suffrage in the
nation.
                    DORA
Mmm. You learn quick. Would you like to meet our
president?
                    ALICE
Yes, absolutely, as long as she's not busy.

Dora smiles and leads her over to ANNA SHAW (60).

                    DORA
She won't be busy when it comes to you. People are ready
to *make* time for you.

Anna is the first woman to spot Alice and not look delightfully
pleased to see her.
                    ANNA
Hello, Miss Paul.

They shake hands.
                    DORA
Alice, this is Anna Shaw. The president of the National
American Woman Suffrage Association.

                    ALICE
Pleased to meet you, Mrs. Shaw.

ANNA
You can call me Anna, child.

She says this, though it's obvious she doesn't mean it.

ALICE
Yes, ma'am.

ANNA
Are you joining us at the Capitol tomorrow?

ALICE
What for?

ANNA
For the annual suffrage hearings before the Senate and House committees.

DORA
Oh, you must! You can ride in my carriage with me, and I'll answer any questions you have about the movement here in America.

Harriot Blatch butts herself into the conversation.

HARRIOT
Alice! Wonderful speech!

ANNA
Harriot, will you be joining us on our voyage to the Capitol tomorrow?

HARRIOT
Absolutely, but, you know, me and mine are mostly focused on obtaining the ballot for the state of New York.

Alice narrows her eyes at this.

HARRIOT (CONT'D)
It is the path toward a federal amendment being passed,
you know.

ANNA
You never did get the chance to take Dora up on her offer,
child.

Alice smiles at Dora.

ALICE
I'd love to pick your brain on the way to D.C.

Harriot's eyes widen on hearing this.

HARRIOT
Do you mind if I steal Alice for a second?

Dora and Anna nod.

ALICE
(to Dora)
Thanks again.

Harriot pulls Alice away from the duo.

HARRIOT
I'd like to make you the Equality League's *first* salaried
political organizer. You are one of the most talented
speakers our movement has, and I want you used
effectively.

ALICE
I really don't want to work toward equality just for the state
of New York. I'd like to work for *national* suffrage.

HARRIOT
That's a bit premature, don't you think? States in the west
are obtaining the right to vote. If New York gets it, we can
easily get a federal amendment passed.

                              ALICE
Well, like I told you, I want to finish school before
extending my energies on woman suffrage, so I can't take
you up on your offer now. Though I do appreciate it.

LUCY BURNS (20s) surprises Alice with a hug. Joy exudes out of
Alice on seeing her.

                              LUCY
Hello, lovely!

                              ALICE
Lucy! Oh my goodness! What a pleasure to see you.
Harriot, this is my dear friend Lucy Burns who was in
England and Scotland with me.

                              LUCY
I was also one of the first American women to be
imprisoned in Scotland for suffrage, but *she* gets all the
attention, doesn't she?

Lucy elbows her playfully. Harriot shifts uncomfortably,
beginning to look like a third wheel.

                            HARRIOT
I suppose I should allow you two to get reacquainted.

                              ALICE
Thank you again for the offer, Harriot.

Harriot nods and leaves them to it. When Harriot's out of earshot,
Lucy quickly turns to Alice.

                              LUCY
Are we going to cause a ruckus over here, too?

Alice grins and nods. Lucy screams with her mouth closed, trying
to suppress her excitement.

ALICE

But we *have* to be smart about it or we won't get anything done.

LUCY

Of course. Of course.

ALICE

And I also have to finish school.

Lucy blows a raspberry. Alice chuckles and glances around.

ALICE (CONT'D)

Shhh! I will be finished in no time.

LUCY

Well, what am I supposed to do until then?

ALICE

I suppose keep your legs closed!

Lucy inhales deeply and feigns slapping Alice's face. They laugh and observe numerous people watching them, so they behave themselves and act like dignified women.

INT. U.S. CAPITOL - DAY

Alice, Dora, and Inez are squeezed into the Senate's hearing room. Anna Shaw is speaking to both houses.

ANNA

It is not revolutionary on our part to ask a share in our government. I have suffrage petitions here...

She holds up the petitions for all to see.

ANNA (CONT'D)

... with 404,825 signatures...

Alice watches the reactions of the men. Some are yawning. Some are checking their watches. Some aren't even listening but talking to each other. Her lips purse at their lack of respect.

FLASHBACK - GUILDHALL

Alice and another suffragist step over to a window.

> ALICE
> If they don't want to listen to us, we'll make them.

She takes off her shoe, breaks the window with it, and sticks her head into the Guildhall while the men inside politick.

> ALICE (CONT'D)
> Votes for women! Votes for women! Votes for women!

BACK TO SCENE

Alice glares at the politicians who are supposed to be FOR the people.

EXT. U.S. CAPITOL - DAY

Greta's holding a bunch of documents and following Congressman Banks. She looks much paler, skinnier, and now has dark circles around her eyes. Her face is a mask of doubt and regret.

Dora, Alice, Inez, and Harriot are standing atop the Capitol steps talking. Inez glares at Congressman Banks and elbows Alice. She whispers to her.

> INEZ
> That's Congressman Banks.

Alice spots him.

> ALICE
> We're going to find a replacement for him.

Anna Shaw slides up to them with a smirk and chest poked out.

                         ANNA
          Same time next year, ladies?

Harriot, Dora, and Inez nod. Alice doesn't. She shakes her head.

                         ALICE
          This is all we're doing on a national level? Once a year
          petition the government to act on woman suffrage?

                         ANNA
          Young lady, what more do you expect us to do? We don't
          want to pester government officials or it may take us
          longer to win the right to vote.

                         HARRIOT
          We don't want to be boxed into the stereotype of being
          nagging women, either.

Alice keeps her mouth shut, but her expression says it all: she
disagrees with these two. Inez reads Alice and rubs her back. Alice
grins at Inez in appreciation.

EXT. UNIVERSITY OF PENNSYLVANIA - DAY

Alice walks toward her school clutching her college books and
materials. Three JOCKS walk past her smiling.

                         JOCK #1
          I didn't know there were ironing classes here.

The jocks laugh. Alice looks around. It appears she is the only lady
on campus.

                         JOCK #2
          What's *she* gonna do with a degree?

Jock #3 closes his eyes and waves his hands in front of her like a psychic might when reading someone.

JOCK #3
I see in your future... clothes being folded... food being cooked... a man being attended to...

JOCK #1
Yeah, you shouldn't be wasting your time here, sweetheart.

Alice picks up her step and walks past them and into the school.

MONTAGE - ALICE'S STUDIES AND PLANNING

— — Alice has a street-corner meeting with over a hundred people attending.

— — Alice studies in her room.

— — Alice obtains a permit for her rally at Independence Square.

— — Alice studies in a library with open books all around her.

— — Alice speaks to hundred's of women at City Hall Plaza, and appears exhausted.

END MONTAGE

EXT. INDEPENDENCE SQUARE - DAY

Thousands of people are gathered at the birthplace of liberty listening to Inez Milholland speak. Alice is off to the side with Lucy looking out at the thousands of people she helped assemble for the rally. She smiles.

Anna steps up to her.
ANNA
You should be very proud of everything you did here today.

                    ALICE
I'm more proud of these women who are beginning to find
their voices.

                    ANNA
I wasn't too sure about you at first. You're just so very
young, but you've proven yourself to be a very competent
leader.

                    ALICE
Thank you.

                    ANNA
I hear your graduation is next month. Any idea what you're
going to do?

                    ALICE
Well, I want to push for a federal suffrage amendment. My
eyes are on a national scale while everyone else's seem to
be focused on their home states. I *have* found people with
the same view as me, even prominent women, but I have
yet to find a suffrage group who desires to go down this
path.

Anna gauges her.
                    ANNA
We currently have a Congressional Committee.

                    ALICE
Which is inactive throughout the year.

Anna grins, impressed that she's done her homework.

                    ANNA
You must have a plan. Let's hear it.

                    ALICE
First thing I want to do is create a national procession in
Washington D.C. with every suffrage group in the U.S.

ANNA
We don't have the money for such grandiose ideas.

ALICE
My friend Lucy and I...

Alice snaps her fingers at Lucy and waves her over. Lucy steps up.
Anna takes her measure.

ALICE (CONT'D)
We can gather the funds needed and set up everything
ourselves. You won't have to worry about anything.

Anna doesn't seem very impressed with Lucy.

ALICE (CONT'D)
She played a vital role in this rally and has the same
experience as me.

ANNA
(nods)
Oh, yes, Lucy Burns. Your partner in crime. Literally...
Hmmm. If I'm to bring you both into the National, I expect
you to leave the criminality back in England.

LUCY/ALICE
Of course!

ANNA
Right. Well, I'll take this up with the board. You...
(points at Alice)
... will be the chair of the Congressional Committee — —
(cuts Alice off)
I've heard about your aversion for the spotlight, and I'm
not having it. Now both of you thank me for making you
members of the National American Woman Suffrage
Association.

                          LUCY/ALICE
                          (hesitant)
          Thank you.

EXT. UNIVERSITY OF PENNSYLVANIA - DAY

One graduate in cap and gown takes the stage to accept his diploma. The audience applauds.

                          DEAN
          Alice Paul.

Dora, Lucy, and Inez make the most noise for Alice even above her mom and Parry. But because there's a large amount of women in the crowd, Alice receives the loudest and most deafening applause.

Alice waves at them.

INT. DORA'S CARRIAGE - DAY

Lucy, Inez, and Alice are giddy with the start of a new adventure. They ride along talking excitedly.

                          INEZ
          Dora's the best, isn't she? Setting us up with the carriage
          and office in D.C.

                          LUCY
          Yeah, and she also gave me a list of names and addresses
          of people we should approach about helping us with
          funding. Here.

Lucy hands Alice the list. Alice reads over it and snaps her head up.
                          ALICE
          Nina Allender? The artist?

Lucy smiles and nods. Alice returns to reading the list.

ALICE (CONT'D)
Alva Belmont? But she's in New York.

LUCY
Yeah, there are people from all over the country. All in support of woman suffrage.

Alice reads on, in awe of the names. She sees a category titled "MONTANA" and eyes Inez.

ALICE
This says, "Jeannette Rankin as possible candidate to replace Congressman Banks."

Inez only nods and stares steely-eyed at Alice.

ALICE (CONT'D)
We'll put aside a separate fund just for her campaign.

INEZ
We should also save up some money so that we can go out there and push for her candidacy.

All three women look at each other with a tremendous amount of strength in their eyes.
LUCY
She'll be the first woman in Congress if we can help make it happen.

The carriage hits a big bump. Alice moves the curtain to peek out the window. And there's the Washington Monument.

ALICE
Well, let's set about doing what's never been done.

EXT. MISS ALLENDER'S HOME - DAY

Alice walks up to the house and knocks on the door. NINA ALLENDER and her MOM answer. Nina is behind her mother. Alice stares straight at Nina.

> ALICE
> Nina Allender, my name is Alice Paul.

> NINA
> We know who you are.

> ALICE
> I'm a big fan of your work and — —

> NINA
> — — And I of yours.

> NINA'S MOTHER
> We both are.

Alice smiles.

> ALICE
> I'm here because I want to take the fight for the ballot to Washington, and I'm hoping to secure funds for the undertaking.

SERIES OF SHOTS - ALICE'S FUNDRAISING

(A)   Alice knocks on a door.

(B)   She talks to some women.

(C)   Alice knocks on another door.

(D)   She talks to some women.

(E)   Someone hands her some money.

(F)   A woman hands her a check.

(G)   A man gives her a bag of change.

END SERIES OF SHOTS

INT. C.C. HEADQUARTERS - DAY

Alice steps through the Congressional Committee's door. Lucy turns to her and grabs a stack of mail. There are a couple women in the office working. Alice eyes them with skepticism.

> LUCY
> All this mail has come in for us during the past couple days.

Lucy hands Alice the mail.
> ALICE
> Who are these women?

Lucy is confused at first.
> LUCY
> Oh them? They work for us now. *Volunteering.* The word is out about what we're doing and many want to help. That's what all this mail is.

> ALICE
> Wanting to help how?

> LUCY
> In all sorts of ways! Volunteer, send money, and one woman wants to help us start our own magazine!

> ALICE
> Wow.

An older lady named HELEN GARDENER (60s) steps into the office and takes off her coat and hat at the door. Lucy leans closer to Alice and whispers to her.

                              LUCY
She's a board member, so be careful around her.

Helen walks up to Alice.

                             HELEN
There she is! Alice, my name is Helen Gardener. I'm here
to help and oversee activities for the procession.

They shake hands.
                        HELEN (CONT'D)
I just spoke with the chief of police about securing a permit
for our demonstration. He doesn't like your date of March
3rd or our destination on Pennsylvania Avenue.

Alice's eyes narrow at Lucy then back at Helen.

                             ALICE
Did he say why?

                             HELEN
The day is bad because it's the day before the president's
inauguration, isn't it? He doesn't like the street, he says,
due to there being saloons at the lower end of Pennsylvania
Avenue. He believes there may be trouble for us.

                              LUCY
We can always go to his superior, District
Commissioner John Johnson.

                             ALICE
We'll show up with well-connected people, too.

                             HELEN
"We'll"?

                             ALICE
Yes, all three of us.

                         HELEN
Anna gave *me* the job specifically to obtain this permit,
young lady.
                         ALICE
And I suspect you're not about to fold now due to one man
in your way. It's time to show up in force and let them see
we're not backing down.

Helen's eyes stab icicles into Alice's. When she opens her mouth,
Alice speaks up.
                    ALICE (CONT'D)
You can take credit for the permit if you want. I don't care
about any of that. I merely want to see this through to the
end.

Helen's shock is almost comical, like Alice just slapped her across
the face.

                         HELEN
Neither am I searching for any praise. Young lady, I am a
board member of the NAWSA.

                         ALICE
I know who you are, ma'am. Now. Shall we jump back in
the fight?

Alice nods to her own question and heads straight for her desk to
begin writing letters. Helen stares after her in wonder. Lucy
whispers to Helen.
                         LUCY
She's something, isn't she?

Helen catches her breath and places a hand over her heart.

                         HELEN
Yes. Very much so.

INT. DISTRICT COMMISSIONER'S OFFICE - DAY

Helen, Nina Allender, Alice, Lucy, and Inez sit on the other side of JOHN JOHNSON'S desk. They glare at him as he speaks to them like children.

JOHNSON

It's not going to happen, ladies. The rif-raf of the South is going to be there in *droves* to toast the Virginia-born Woodrow Wilson. Why not have your parade later in the spring and on a more respectable road like Sixteenth Street? It *exudes* propriety and wealth! Much more fit for *ladies* like yourselves.

He winks at them. Lips purse at the bastard.

ALICE

That doesn't work for us. Everything about what we're trying to do is political. Pennsylvania Avenue is a *political* street. It connects the house of Congress and the presidential mansion. And March 3rd is the eve of the presidential inauguration—that real and metaphorical transfer of power. It sends the message that women are here at the gates, ready to enter the political realm.

JOHNSON

What about March 5th, the day after the inauguration?

ALICE

You want us to send a metaphorical message that we're *late*, Mr. Johnson? No, it should be that we're *ready, now,* and *waiting*. We don't want the vote tomorrow. We wanted it yesterday. The day before. Do you understand?

Johnson sighs.

JOHNSON

I'm sorry. It can't be done.
(stands)
Now let me see you ladies out.

He walks over to his office door and opens it. The women hesitate before exiting.

INT. C.C. HEADQUARTERS – DAY

Alice, Helen, Lucy, and Inez step into the office. Only Alice doesn't appear defeated.

HELEN
We need to change the date. He will give us Pennsylvania Avenue, I think. We only need to change the date.

ALICE
We need the date of March the 3rd because more people will be there, and we will generate more publicity with that date. And more publicity means more money for Jeannette Rankin's campaign.

Alice paces the room, thinking.

ALICE (CONT'D)
We have yet to grant any newspapers an interview. We'll do so now. The four of us will describe our *fight* for the day and street.
INEZ
Reporters love a story with conflict.

LUCY
And we'll give them one.

ALICE
I'm going to lobby House and Senate officials about this, too. We're not giving in.

INT. WASHINGTON TIMES - DAY

Alice sits with a REPORTER.

ALICE
There is no reason why we should not have Pennsylvania Avenue since men's processions have always marched there.

INT. WASHINGTON TIMES - DAY

Alice talks with another JOURNALIST.

ALICE
We want to do this on Pennsylvania Avenue because it connects the house of Congress and the presidential mansion. It's the quintessential channel of American political might.

INT. RESTAURANT - DAY

Alice speaks with several reporters at once.

ALICE
There are many members of Congress who fully support our place and date for procession. They understand. Why can't John Johnson?

INT. C.C. HEADQUARTERS - DAY

Newspaper after newspaper after newspaper is slapped down on top of a table. One headline reads "THE FIGHT IS ON!" Another says "WOMEN WANT MORE." The last declares "PERMIT GRANTED!"

Alice, Helen, Lucy, and Inez raise glasses of champagne with the MANY volunteers now.

ALICE
To winning one battle and smiling at the war ahead.

Cheers and hoots follow. Then drinking.

EXT. PENNSYLVANIA AVENUE - DAY

SUPER: March 3rd, 1913

The women and men (mostly women) march down Pennsylvania Avenue. Out in front on a white charger is Inez Milholland wearing a white suit and boots and a blue cape. A gold tiara adorns her long dark hair.

A wagon rolls behind Inez with a sign reading "WE DEMAND AN AMENDMENT TO THE UNITED STATES CONSTITUTION ENFRANCHISING THE WOMEN OF THE COUNTRY."

After the "Great Demand" float is a section of marchers and floats representing countries where women can vote. Floats in the second section illustrate the suffrage struggle from 1840, 1870, 1890, and 1913.

A third section demonstrates the ways women help build a strong state. On one float, a man bearing the state on his shoulders stands alongside a woman in handcuffs. "Man needs her help but she cannot give it," a legend reads above them.

One section features college women in academic gowns. Alice stands in this group. On each side of her is a woman of color. There's a sense of togetherness here, of sisterhood. One YOUNG GIRL (11) looks on in awe.

They march block after block. Men begin to shout profanities at the women. Police officers who are supposed to be keeping the onlookers back laugh. When the men see the officers find their antics funny, they grow braver.

The Young Girl looks frightened, first for the women, then for herself as men around her become aggressive as well.

The bullies taunt them, snatch their banners away, spit on them, and even stop some. Chaos erupts. Inez uses her white charger to run down a man who slapped a woman. The man's knocked down. The Young Girl standing on the sidelines watching gapes with pride at Inez.

The horse stomps on one of the man's legs. He screams. His leg is crushed. Inez charges after other unruly men.

Alice sees men attacking women and goes back and forth between reality and flashbacks of when fifty thousand other women stormed Parliament — where women were being attacked by officers.

She's on the verge of having a complete breakdown. She breathes in deep controlled breaths. Slowly, very slowly, she regains command of her senses and spots a police officer. She runs up to him.

ALICE
Do your job! These people need to be pulled back.

OFFICER
Little lady, you have no idea what my job entails.

Alice groans and pushes a man who grabs at her. He's a running molester, running around grabbing at women. Some men come to their aid, pushing the other men back. Women fight alongside them.

The running molester is happily getting his fill of perversion when he runs right into a kick in the nuts. The Young Girl retreats back into the crowd after doing her part.

Men and women in the crowd start to regain control. Anna Shaw watches Alice help maintain order. Her eyes narrow on the possible rival to her leadership. She says something to Helen standing beside her. The procession is now able to march peacefully past the White House.

INT. C.C. HEADQUARTERS - DAY

Alice walks into the place and all heads turn to her. She's grinning like an insane person. Helen, Lucy, and Inez are excited to see what she has for them.

ALICE
Because of our successful procession, I secured us a meeting with the *president*!

All cheer except Helen.

HELEN
Did you discuss this with Anna?

ALICE
You all are the first to know.

INEZ
She did just walk through the door.

HELEN
She should know what you're doing.

LUCY
She knows what we're doing. She sent us!

HELEN
You are much too young to be meeting with the president. You'll likely say something foolhardy.

The "young" women glare at Helen, except Alice.

ALICE
Obviously you will accompany us, so what's the bother?

Helen folds her arms over her chest.

HELEN
I most certainly am not. I'm going to notify Anna about this straight away and get it quashed. We cannot have you sullying the NAWSA name by representing us.

LUCY
Then we will represent ourselves when we speak with the president.

HELEN
I'm going to see to it that you don't speak to the president at all!

She heads straight out of there. The women take each other in, wondering what that was all about.

EXT. WHITE HOUSE - DAY

Alice walks up to the White House with Dora, Lucy, and Inez. Their posture, their strides, their countenances are full of confidence.

INT. WHITE HOUSE - DAY

The four women step into the oval Office. The president of the United States, WOODROW WILSON, shakes their hands and exchanges pleasantries.

PRESIDENT
Quite a buzz you all made with your demonstration. The press was talking about it for *weeks*. Very clever keeping your cause in the headlines.

He gestures for them to sit. All take a seat.

DORA
Thank you, Mr. President.

ALICE

President Wilson, we're here today about the Anthony Amendment I wrote.

PRESIDENT
(surprise)
That *you* wrote? Oh yes, you're the one that obtained a doctorate in political science, aren't you?

This was stated as more of a rhetorical question, so Alice doesn't answer.

ALICE

I'm dubbing it the Anthony Amendment to honor Susan B. Anthony. It was her desire to see a federal suffrage amendment passed, and with the Democrats controlling both the House and Senate, I believe with your encouragement they can get this bill passed.

PRESIDENT

I didn't run on this issue, so I feel like my hands are tied. The people have spoken, but not on woman suffrage.

INEZ

Mr. President, the paramount issue of the day is woman suffrage.

PRESIDENT

I'm sorry, but Congress has more pressing matters: currency, tariff reform — —

ALICE

— — But, Mr. President, do you not understand that the administration has no right to legislate currency, tariff, or any other reform without first getting the consent of women?

PRESIDENT

Ladies... I will consider your views.
(stands)
I think that will be all for today.

ALICE

We were only afforded ten minutes of your time, and we couldn't even have that.

The women stand.

LUCY

Mr. President, one last word... Several million women now vote in nine states. Consider wisely.

They exit the room.

EXT. WHITE HOUSE – DAY

Inez, Lucy, and Dora are red-faced as they leave the White House. Alice on the other hand is stoic.

ALICE

He says it's the people who have decided. Well, I say we find a candidate who *wants* to help.

INT. C.C. HEADQUARTERS - DAY

Newspapers from over the weeks lay scattered about on a table. Pen marks circle "Anna Shaw charges Alice Paul with over aggressiveness," "Anna Shaw sets to remove Miss Paul from Congressional Committee," and other lines on Anna attacking Alice.

Alice sits with Dora, Lucy, and Inez.

LUCY

We have enough people backing us. We don't need them.

ALICE

We've raised more money than they *ever* have for national work. They *have* to see the people are behind us.

INEZ

This whole board meeting to remove you only divides us, prevents us from focusing on the fight for the ballot.

DORA

Word is Anna's going to have the NAWSA's former president Carrie Catt there for support.

Inez gasps and turns to Alice with pity in her eyes.

INEZ

Mrs. Catt is the matriarch for woman suffrage.

LUCY

Maybe it's time to start thinking of our own suffrage group. They don't like what we're doing? Okay. Bye!

ALICE

I'm not even sure if it's what we're doing she doesn't like. She reproved me for speaking with the president. Then she turns around and visits with the president herself. I write a federal amendment, and she has someone write one for her.

DORA

Which everyone agrees is inferior to yours.

ALICE

But my point is, she's copying all of my moves as if she can do better. Undermining me.

LUCY

More like she's threatened by you. You're making power moves nonstop, and she's been sitting for forty years. You're showing how irrelevant and dated her methods are.

Alice shifts in her seat, uncomfortable with the praise.

ALICE

Regardless, we need the NAWSA's connections, support, and political power. Look how quickly they got that joke of a bill to the Senate floor.

INEZ

I could ask Harriot to support you in the meeting.

LUCY

And she has clout.

ALICE

I'm not going down without a fight.

INEZ

I'll wire her a message, then.

LUCY

Now let's *consider* a new organization. One we'll lead ourselves.

Alice thinks about it. She nods.

INT. NAWSA HEADQUARTERS - DAY

Anna, Dora, CARRIE CATT (54), JANE ADAMS (50s), Helen, and a couple other women sit behind a long table. A good ten feet away sit Alice, Lucy, Inez, and Harriot Blatch.

ANNA

I first want to thank everyone for meeting with us today. We're here to discuss removing Alice Paul from the NAWSA due to a number of reasons. First, Miss Paul's attacks on the president and on the Democrat party are un-American and militant. We at the NAWSA stand proudly nonpartisan, and we shall always help our friends. Unless she chooses to stop these attacks, I move to dismiss her as a member of the NAWSA altogether.

JANE
What say you, Miss Paul?

HARRIOT
Doctor Paul would be more respectful.

ALICE
That's okay. As for my attack on the governing party, it's justified as far as I'm concerned. The Democrats are the one's in power. The Democrats are the ones suppressing not only *our* right to vote but the Negroes right to vote, too. Who controls the Senate? The Democrats. Who's the more progressive party? The Republicans. If we can have the Republicans on our side ALONG with the few Democrats who are already on our side, we'll have firmer ground to stand on. Democrats will indeed feel the pressure to pass a federal suffrage amendment with this strategy. If not, they risk losing seats.

The women on the board nod. They like it. Anna cuts in before she loses them to Alice.
ANNA
Your amendment was so faulty I had to have Ruth McCormick write one for us.

Harriot laughs out loud.

HARRIOT
I read your Shafroth Amendment, and it is utterly ridiculous. Embarrassing, really.

ANNA
(to Alice)
You have also been very divisive by calling me a "dear old lady."
ALICE
Neither I nor anyone in the Committee has responded to any of the criticisms of us made by *you*, so why should we start now? Whatever you read is false.

HARRIOT
You have been divisive, Anna. This woman has less than one percent of the NAWSA's membership, yet she's raised more than half the monies in one year than the National ever has. You're threatened by her. Admit it.

Anna sits firmly in her seat.

ANNA
Where did you get that information?

HARRIOT
You're not the only one with friends, Anna.

Carrie stands to meet Alice's eyes and a venerable silence and stillness falls into the room.

CARRIE
Miss Paul, I am Carrie Catt. We are all patriots here at the National. That's what you are not comprehending. We do not attack our government. That is the mark of an anarchist. How are you going to attack something you claim you want to be part of? Your actions make us look like foolish women who are better served in the kitchen than in Congress, which is exactly what we here at the NAWSA want to avoid. So I call on all the board to raise your hands with me if you agree in removing Alice Paul as a member of the NAWSA.

Dora and Jane do not raise their hands, but all the rest of the women do. Majority rules. Alice's chin holds firmly raised. Lucy, Harriot, and Inez stand with Alice.

LUCY
We will start our own organization then, and we'll be sure to keep a tally of all the defectors from the NAWSA who join us.

As Lucy, Harriot, Inez, and Alice start for the exit, Dora stands.

                        DORA
I'd like to be the first defector.

                        JANE
I'm tired of being quiet and patient while men walk all over
us.

Jane stands, too. She and Dora walk toward the small group. Inez
smirks at the board.
                        INEZ
Two before we've even walked out of the door. I do believe
this will be a remarkable turnout.

                        LUCY
Be sure to read our new magazine *The Suffragist* to
keep track of the numbers of defectors.

Lucy winks at Anna.

EXT. NAWSA HEADQUARTERS - DAY

Alice and her gals exit the NAWSA headquarters. Dora sidles up
to Alice.
                        DORA
What's next?

                        ALICE
What's next is we don't look back. We focus on
enfranchisement.

                        LUCY
And when they attack us?

                        ALICE
We ignore them. Their goal may be to degrade us and bring
us down, but *our goal* is to win the ballot.

The grit and determination in her eyes shows us she means it. Those eyes have a singular focus.

INT. U.S. CAPITOL – DAY

Lucy, Dora, Inez, and Alice are lobbying four congressmen separately. Inez has Congressman Banks. They passionately plead their cases while the congressmen's backs are literally against the wall.

> INEZ
> The idea of going to war is being kicked around to win the freedom for peoples in other nations, but what about the women in *your* country? When are you going to grant us *our* freedom?

Against another wall, Alice grills a congressman.

> ALICE
> We at the National Woman's Party are calling on ALL women and men to campaign against any congressman who shifts responsibility off of themselves when it comes to woman suffrage. When you go back to Ohio, you *will* be met with people asking you where you stand and how you plan to act. We have members of the NWP in every state.

> CONGRESSMAN
> I heard you're trying to remove all Democrats.

> ALICE
> No. All congressmen are being lobbied exactly like you are, and they will soon find themselves out of a job like you will if you don't start standing up for what's right.

EXT. BILLINGS, MONTANA - DAY

Alice is standing on a large platform with JEANNETTE RANKIN (30s) speaking to a couple hundred men and women. A sign behind her says, "LET'S VOTE FOR RANKIN, MONTANA." And who's standing in the crowd looking up at Alice with hope-filled eyes but Greta Graham.

ALICE

A new day has come! The National Woman's Party has all of its support in Jeannette Rankin here.

(gestures at her)

Congressman Banks isn't for freedom, isn't for democracy, which is why we're asking Jeannette Rankin to lead us into the future!

Cheers and whistles ring out.

EXT. HELENA, MONTANA – DAY

Congressman Banks is on the hustings, making a speech before a large crowd. Greta miserably stands off to the side of the stage.

BANKS

These little women think *I* hold all the power!

(laughs)

They don't even realize I'm *one man*! An entire body of people control Congress. Not I alone! Now is this who you want in the House? Some *woman* who doesn't even know how legislation is passed?

EXT. GREAT FALLS, MONTANA - DAY

Jeannette Rankin has now taken the stage. Alice stands on the sidelines watching. Greta is walking through the crowd to get to Alice.

JEANNETTE

Congressman Banks would like you to believe I don't know anything other than how to fold clothes, iron, and cook. But I graduated college. And with higher scores than him!

People in the crowd laugh.

JEANNETTE (CONT'D)
He'll have you believe I don't know my left hand from my right. If that's how he views me, *a human being*, how do you suppose he sees you hard working people without the same education as him? As less than, I'd assume. Now a woman? I come to you with a mother's unconditional love. I only want the best for you. I could NEVER look down on you.

Greta approaches Alice.
GRETA
Excuse me, Miss Paul?

Alice turns and acknowledges her with a look.

GRETA (CONT'D)
Hi, my name is Greta Gra - -

ALICE
- - I know exactly who you are. At first I figured you were spying on our rallies for your boss, but after observing your looks of gratitude for what we were saying, I thought, "We may convert this one yet."

Alice grins and winks at her. Greta gapes.

GRETA
You really got the measure of everything and everyone, don't you?
ALICE
You come to me because you want to switch sides?

Greta nods, in awe of the genius of this woman.

ALICE (CONT'D)
If you really want to help our cause, stay with him. Feed him false information. Tell him our crowds hate it when

ALICE (CONT'D)
Jeannette speaks of the work ethic of women, that crowds turn on her.

A spark comes into Greta's eyes. She understands how invaluable she can really be. She nods and smiles. This is the first time we've seen Greta smile since the first scene she was in.

ALICE (CONT'D)
I'll keep you posted on any other ideas I have.

GRETA
You know how to contact me?

ALICE
Of course.

EXT. MISSOULA, MONTANA - DAY

Congressman Banks projects a calm, jovial exterior, but there's a sense of inner turmoil in his words, a desperation to be heard and believed.

BANKS
What does this *woman* know about hard work, I used to cut trees in my teens and twenties like the rest of you! Where's her calluses and scars? I have mine!

He shows his hands to the crowd. A couple men chuckle but the majority grumble. One LUMBERJACK in the front shouts at him.

LUMBERJACK
My mother was a hardworking single parent.

ANOTHER
Yeah! Watch your mouth, Banks!

Banks forces an unsure smile on his face.

EXT. NWP HEADQUARTERS - DAY

The National Woman's Party doesn't just have an office; it has a *house*. There is a flag that hangs proudly outside of it. It's purple, white, and gold with nine gold stars representing the nine free states.

Dora steps up to the NWP headquarters.

INT. NWP HEADQUARTERS - DAY

Dora walks into a party. Champagne is being passed around. Inez, Lucy, and Alice all appear very tired. Alice and Inez are very thin and pale, but they're wearing big smiles. Volunteers are everywhere.

ALICE

Somebody grab the flag so we can sew on two more stars!

Lucy hoots, and one woman runs outside to grab the NWP flag. Dora sits next to Alice.

DORA

When was the last time you ate, honey?

ALICE

I eat every day, woman, but now is the time for celebration!

DORA

Yes, Nevada and Montana won suffrage. I know.

LUCY

Congressman Banks doesn't stand a chance against us now.

INEZ

We also got twenty-three freedom hating Democrats out of office! And Banks is next!

Alice, Inez, and Lucy raise their glasses to that and drink. Dora grabs Alice's glass.

ALICE

Hey!

DORA

You shouldn't drink on an empty stomach.

Dora takes in the three women. Her lip trembles. She bursts out of her chair.

DORA (CONT'D)

You women are overworking yourselves!

The celebrating stops. The woman who went outside to grab the flag comes back into a room that now has a different mood and doesn't realize it.

FLAG WOMAN

That flag was a stubborn bastard coming off there.

She sees the vibe in the room has changed and glances around.

FLAG WOMAN (CONT'D)

What I miss?

The trio stands by Dora's side. She's weak in the knees. They help her sit back down.

DORA

You ladies are *killing* yourselves! Don't you see that!?

LUCY

Give us a day's rest and we'll look ten times better, just you watch.

DORA

No! You ladies are going to listen to me from now on. You're going to stop your work and eat when I say and sleep when I say.

ALICE

It's been a struggle to — —

                          DORA
— — I won't have it!

Women chuckle. Dora's shocked expression due to the laughter
causes Alice to snicker as well.

                     DORA (CONT'D)
I'm serious! In fact, I'm going to make you all a meal right
now.

Dora stands and heads for the kitchen. Another woman comes in
with needle, thread, and two stars for the flag. Alice grabs the flag,
sits, and gets to work sewing the stars on.

EXT. NWP HEADQUARTERS - NIGHT

Alice sits alone out on the balcony staring up at the moon and
stars. Inez steps out to join her.

                          INEZ
May I join you? Or would you like to be alone?

                          ALICE
No, I'd appreciate some company.

Inez takes a seat beside her. They quietly gaze upon the stars.

                          INEZ
You know, I've been wanting to thank you for a while now.
                    (Alice eyes her)
I've been doing this for a long time, but since you came into
the fight, it's felt like this can really happen. I've never been
more hopeful. I feel like I'll actually see it during my
lifetime. How many others didn't, you know?

Alice nods.
                          ALICE
Susan B. Anthony.

Inez nods. They sit in silence again, staring up into the heavens where all the retired suffragists rest.

INT. NWP HEADQUARTERS - ALICE'S ROOM - NIGHT

Alice is having another nightmare. She's tossing and turning and moaning.

DREAM/FLASHBACK - ALICE IN PRISON

A naked Alice slips in and out of consciousness as she's being carried by several guards. They make it to a chair where she is strapped down into it. A DOCTOR shoves a tube down her throat and force feeds her.

BACK TO SCENE

Alice awakes, sweating and exhausted. She's shivering and on the verge of crying, but she does exactly what she did at the procession: she takes deep calming breaths. Again, after many breaths, she relaxes and lies back down. This time she falls into a peaceful sleep.

INT. NWP HEADQUARTERS - MORNING

Alice steps into the dining room to see Dora has prepared breakfast. Lucy and Inez are eating while sharing a newspaper. Lucy is about to turn the page but Inez stops her by placing a hand on top of hers.

DORA

Alice, dear, have a seat. I'll make you a plate.

Alice sits. Inez releases Lucy's hand and the page turns.

LUCY
(reading)

"After refusing to consider suffrage for nearly a year, the House Rules Committee agreed to report out the Anthony Amendment."

ALICE

Let me see.

Alice rises and aims to snatch the paper away, but Inez and Lucy force her back.

LUCY

You will wait your turn.

Alice's mind races. It's in her eyes. What should their next move be? How can they prepare? What must they do to gain leverage? Inez and Lucy continue reading.

When Dora arrives with Alice's plate, she's gone. Dora's eyebrows nearly touch.

DORA

Where did Alice go?

Inez shrugs. Lucy shakes her head. Dora marches over to Inez and pushes her plate of food closer to her.

DORA (CONT'D)

You can eat and read at the same time. I want that plate cleared, you hear me? No excuses about it being cold. That'd be your fault.

Inez shovels food into her mouth so she can return to reading. Her cheeks are stuffed with food like a chipmunk's. She reads, chews, and swallows little chunks at a time.

Dora hunts for Alice while carrying her plate of food. She finds her in her room writing a letter. Without checking behind her, Alice knows it's Dora.

ALICE

The Democrats are going to kill off the two national proposals as quickly as they can. We have to gather as many women as possible to help us lobby the president for his support.

Dora sighs, pulls up a chair, and sits beside Alice. She scoops some food onto a spoon and brings it to Alice's lips. She looks at it curiously for a second and opens her mouth.

Dora quietly feeds her as she writes.

EXT. WHITE HOUSE – DAY

Dozens of women stand outside the White House wearing purple, white, and gold. They're waving NWP flags. Alice speaks with REPORTERS.

ALICE

We have women of all sorts out here: congressmen's wives, socialites like Alva Belmont, and — —

REPORTER

— — And doctors like yourself.

ALICE

Women of *all* classes. We're not brandishing hostility. We're seeking hospitality. We want in. We're tired of being outsiders in our own country.

Reporters write down her words.

JOURNALIST

What do you think about what the president said earlier?

ALICE

And what was that?

He reads from a notepad.

JOURNALIST

He said, "Suffrage for women will make absolutely no change in politics. It is the home that will be disastrously affected. Somebody has to make the house, and who is going to do it if the women don't?"

Alice and a couple of other women overhearing the statement ball their fists or turn red-faced.

ALICE
Did I say we were out here without hostility? Scratch that. I am very angry. That's all I have to say.
(to women)
Ladies! I do believe the president wants us in the kitchen. There's no reason for us to be out here braving the cold for a man's support that we're never going to receive.

REPORTER
Does this mean you're giving up the fight for woman's suffrage?
ALICE
No. It's simply time to shift tactics.

INT. U.S. CAPITOL - DAY

Alice and a great many women are packed in the U.S. Capitol listening to the congressmen debate over suffrage for women.

CONGRESSMAN #1
Women must be protected against themselves.

Alice and other women write down the quote, his name, and political party. This one? "Democrat."

SERIES OF SHOTS - CONGRESSMEN DEBATE

(A) A congressman takes a sympathetic approach.

CONGRESSMAN #2
I have nothing but respect, admiration, and reverence for womanhood, but I cannot stand by while she becomes degraded by the vote.

(B) Congressman Banks speaks.

                              BANKS
I don't know *ANY* man who would marry a suffragist. Not
any sane one at least.

                          CONGRESSMEN
Boo! Your own mother is a suffragist, you vile wretch! Sit
down!

Banks looks around like he doesn't get these guys. The women
don't need to write on their notepads. He's already a target.

(C) A GOOD CONGRESSMAN debates.

                       GOOD CONGRESSMAN
I believe in freedom, and I don't understand the
Democrats' desire to suppress our countrywomen.

Women nod and applaud.

END SERIES OF SHOTS

EXT. U.S. CAPITOL - DAY

Alice, Lucy, Inez, Dora, and other women exit the Capitol. All the
women appear disappointed. All except Alice, that is. She's
smiling while reading the names. Dora notices her glee and stops
her.
                              DORA
How can you smile after that? We lost the vote.

                              ALICE
Yes, but it proves we're right to go after the Democrats.
They comprised 171 of the 204 nay votes, *and* we have all
their names. Many of them were claiming to be on the
fence. Here we have the truth. They're now very vulnerable
targets.

She gives Dora an evil grin.

INEZ
I thought we weren't specifically targeting Democrats?

ALICE
We're not. We're targeting 171 of them and
33 Republicans.

INEZ
It does get confusing, you know.

Alice smiles.

ALICE
No, you just want to tease me.

DORA
All right, let's find some lunch.

The trio laughs at Dora and her motherliness. Dora shakes her head and waves them to follow her.

INT. NWP HEADQUARTERS – DAY

At least a couple dozen women stand around in groups of five reading newspapers. Inez reads one aloud for the women around her.

INEZ
"Though the amendment failed to reach the required two-thirds majority, legislators took notice of the historic vote brought about by the National Woman's Party."

A couple women suppress their giddiness. Lucy is also quietly reading out loud for a group of women.

LUCY
"If the NAWSA shifted their energies from attacking Miss Paul's character to working on suffrage, they might actually accomplish as much as Miss Paul has."

Alice isn't in any of these groups. She's off to the side reading a newspaper by herself. Nobody's interested in what she's reading because the headline reads "PANAMA-PACIFIC EXPOSITION." Dora makes her way over to Alice.

                              DORA
          What are you reading there?

                              ALICE
          It's the world's fair commemorating the end of the construction of the Panama Canal.

                              DORA
          Ready to stage some more political theater, are you?

Alice glances up at her.
                              ALICE
          We cannot continue doing the same things like the NAWSA. We have to find *NEW WAYS* of bringing woman suffrage to the headlines. This issue has to *stay* in the nation's consciousness.

                              DORA
          The last world's fair drew millions of visitors, if I'm not mistaken. This could be huge for us.

                              ALICE
          Nineteen million. I *will* get us a booth there.

                              DORA
          I know you will.

Dora kisses the top of her head.

                         DORA (CONT'D)
          I'm going to prepare dinner.

Alice returns to reading the newspaper.

INT. WORLD'S FAIR – DAY

Upon entering the Panama-Pacific Exposition, the National Woman's Party booth is placed favorably near the fair's entrance. An oval portrait of Susan B. Anthony hangs prominently. Bouquets decorate the booth.

A map of the United States is also displayed behind them showing the status of woman suffrage in every state. Alice and two other women are greeting everyone who enters, and two other women outside of the booth speak with arrivals.

A WOMAN walks over to Alice.

                    WOMAN
          What a lovely display you have here.

                    ALICE
          Thank you. We're also holding a Women Voters'
          Convention, which will also be lovely. We have here what
          we're calling a grand petition that you can sign supporting
          the Anthony Amendment.

Alice slides her the petition and a pen.

                    WOMAN
          Oh, I've read about the Anthony Amendment. This is the
          good one, right?

Alice can't help but smile.

                    ALICE
          Yes, ma'am. The other one was recently abandoned by its
          creators.

The woman nods.

                    WOMAN
          Anna Shaw had to bow to all the critics of it.

Alice seems impressed by the woman.

WOMAN (CONT'D)
I'm a fan of your magazine. *The Suffragist* is a great read.

ALICE
I appreciate your saying so. You should come to the convention. There will be...

EXT. WOMEN VOTERS' CONVENTION – DAY

SUPER: September 14th, 1915

Lucy is wrapping up a speech to an audience of around a hundred thousand. Reporters and photographers are there to capture the event. Off to the side are three women sitting in a car.

ALICE (V.O.)
... an envoy going on a cross-country mission to drive from here in California to Washington D.C. They're tasked with delivering the grand petition to Congress.

The audience sings as Lucy, Alice, Inez, Dora, Jeannette Rankin, and a dozen other women help carry and load the massive petition into the car.

WOMEN
(singing)
We are women clad in new power.
We refuse to cower.
We march to set our sisters free.
We, too, are human beings!

The hooting and hollering is deafening as the vehicle drives off and passes through the opening gates.

MONTAGE – ENVOY'S TRAVELS

— — The vehicle crawls through a snow storm.

> ALICE (V.O.)
> Those courageous souls will have to brave undoubtedly harsh weather...

— — The women are fixing a flat tire.

> ALICE (V.O.)
> ... breakdowns...

— — The trio is at a servicing station having people sign the petition.

> ALICE (V.O.)
> ... all while collecting more signatures for the Anthony Amendment.

END MONTAGE

INT. TRAIN – DAY

Alice and her posse travel.

> ALICE (V.O,)
> I will travel by train to meet them there.

EXT. WASHINGTON, D.C. STREETS – DAY

The car with the trio and petition in it are directed by tens of thousands of women wearing purple, white, and gold on both sides of every street. The women cheer the car on.

After driving down street after street, the vehicle stops at the White House. Alice, staying out of the spotlight, has Inez, Dora, Lucy, and seventeen other women help carry the petition into the presidential mansion.

INT. WHITE HOUSE – EAST ROOM – DAY

President Woodrow Wilsom smiles as the women enter one by

one into the East Room with the colossal petition.

                    PRESIDENT
This is the most impressive petition I have ever seen.

The women smile, but they also have a guarded demeanor. His remarks on women needing to make the house likely still on their minds.
                    PRESIDENT (CONT'D)
I promise to consider very carefully what is right for us to do.

EXT. WHITE HOUSE – DAY

The women exit the White House, and EDWIN WEBB (50s) follows them out searching the crowd. He spots Alice and walks up to her.
                    EDWIN
I thought you would have joined the women in the White House with the petition.

Alice stares at him.

                    EDWIN (CONT'D)
Apologies. I'm Edwin Webb the House Judiciary Committee Chairman.

Alice nods as soon as he says his name.

                    ALICE
What can I do for you, Mr. Webb?

                    EDWIN
Well, I came out here to tell you we're going to quickly grant you a suffrage hearing in December. How does that sound?

Alice gauges him. Something's up. Dora, Inez, and Lucy feign like they're talking, though they're clearly eavesdropping.

ALICE
I'm very pleased to hear that, but I don't believe that's all you came out here to tell me.

EDWIN
To be frank, you just held one of the biggest and most dramatic suffrage conventions that has probably ever been held in the history of the world. It's been in the headlines for over a month now.

ALICE
And as a Democrat, you're wondering what my plans are moving forward.

EDWIN
You *are* unrelenting.

ALICE
What we do depends on what you do.

Edwin weighs her words and chooses his next ones carefully, slightly hesitating as he says them.

EDWIN
We will come to a better understanding of the situation if we knew what you are going to do to us.

ALICE
You're worried about next year's elections.

They stare each other down.

ALICE (CONT'D)
We just made our move. Now it's yours, but don't hesitate. Procrastination is the one move we won't stand for anymore. Have a good day, Mr. Webb.

Alice turns her back on him and leaves. The ear-hustling trio rushes to her side giggling.

LUCY

You had that bastard by the balls!

INEZ

We have political power now.

DORA

In all my years in this movement, I've never seen anything like that. They *fear* us now.

Alice isn't smiling. None of these words make her happy. It all merely has her face and eyes more determined. Alice stops walking and faces them.

ALICE

Have you all figured out *why* he's afraid yet?
(waits)
It's because he knows his party isn't ready to vote for suffrage. We need to get ready for the presidential campaign.

Alice walks away, leaving the trio standing there doing the math.

INT. NWP HEADQUARTERS – DAY

Lucy walks into the room fanning herself with a letter and chuckling. Inez and Dora look up from their work, but not Alice. She continues to write a letter.

INEZ

What was in the mail that has you so giddy?

Alice's head picks up on that.

LUCY

Good old Mrs. Catt wrote the NWP, and she wants to meet with Alice. She's the new president of the NAWSA.

Inez and Dora Laugh.

DORA
Is it all the members we've stolen from them?

INEZ
Or is it Alice's ingenuity?

LUCY
Or did their ridiculously pathetic attempts to copy every move we make embarrass them to this point?

The three women laugh harder. Even Alice smiles at that. She stands and reaches for the letter.

ALICE
Let me see that.

Lucy hands it to her. As she reads it, Inez chuckles some more.

INEZ
What'd that one reporter say when the papers *blasted* them for trying to duplicate our cross-country drive to the White House? "The NWP should be proud. Imitation is the greatest form of flattery."

LUCY
She and Anna should be ashamed of themselves.

DORA
Their actions were disgraceful.

Inez watches Alice read.

INEZ
Don't tell me you're actually entertaining the idea of meeting with her.

DORA
Why wouldn't she?

INEZ
They're insignificant to us!

LUCY
And we hold more political power than them. Politicians come to *us* for the favor now.

INEZ
I've worked with Harriot, Anna, Carrie Catt, and many others over the years, and I *never* saw politicians come to them in search of support, but I have seen *them* beg for it.

ALICE
As all of us in this room have.

All wait for an answer from her.

ALICE (CONT'D)
I'm going to meet with her. Though she's been acting like a drowning cat, scratching and clawing at us, we can show the same compassion we're seeking from our government.

Dora nods.
DORA
Well said.

ALICE
But I will go alone.
(cuts off objections)
We need to prepare for the upcoming elections. This one's going to be a battle.

INT. NAWSA HEADQUARTERS – DAY

Alice enters the same room she was dismissed from, but now it's not as cold and unwelcoming. There are flowers, lace, and other fine materials decorating the room. Carrie Catt rises out of a chair to greet Alice. Carrie forces a smile.

                    CARRIE
Alice, thank you for coming.

                    ALICE
I appreciate the invitation.

                    CARRIE
Please have a seat.

They sit.
                    CARRIE (CONT'D)
You know I have always felt the same as you in regards to
pushing for a federal amendment.

Alice grins politely.

                    CARRIE (CONT'D)
It appears the majority of the women in this country have
come to see our point of view. Even that vile Harriot Blatch
wants to focus on national suffrage.

                    ALICE
Yes, we work very closely with her, and we'd like to work
with you as well.

Carrie grins like a cat who's caught a mouse.

                    CARRIE
As we with you, my dear. We'd work much better together
than against each other.

                    ALICE
I agree, though I've never been against you.

                    CARRIE
The problem is, this election policy of yours. Threatening
politicians hurts our cause, creates enemies not friends.

ALICE
If they're against woman suffrage, they're already my enemy. Plus, *we* have politicians reaching out to us for endorsements now. We are making plenty of friends.

Carrie scowls at this.

CARRIE
Republicans, no doubt. But we should be nonpartisan.

ALICE
And we are.

CARRIE
Not when you're attacking Democrats.

ALICE
Republicans who are against enfranchisement receive the same treatment, but you know this, so why exactly did you call me out here? If it were simply a means of attempting to control me, I might as well take my leave.

Carrie stands and glares at Alice with such hate it seems insane.

CARRIE
No. I will leave, but know this: *I will fight you to the last ditch.*

With that, Carrie turns her back on Alice and exits the room. Alice sits there like this attempt to bridge the gap between them was a complete waste of her time. She shakes her head and stands.

EXT. NEVADA – DAY

President Woodrow Wilson is on the hustings. He's just finished wrapping up a speech. REPORTERS swarm him.

REPORTER
You sure you won't change your position on federal suffrage for women?

The president's eyes reveal his contempt, but he quickly covers it up with a smile.

PRESIDENT
I believe in states' rights.

JOURNALIST
Those women are fighting like mad against you, going door to door, speaking in every county in all the suffrage states. You're not worried?

PRESIDENT
I don't quite understand what their bother is with me. I voted in New Jersey for woman's suffrage. I'm not against them.

REPORTER
They want your support for their Anthony Amendment.

He stops walking. Everyone can tell the president is about to make a serious statement. The reporters get their pencils and notepads ready for a quote.

PRESIDENT
I'd like to make my first request for *all* to recognize woman suffrage. Yes, I do believe in states' rights, but I also believe each state will do the right thing when the time is good for them.

Reporters write down everything he's said. The president gestures at some men. They walk over and hold the reporters back.

PRESIDENT (CONT'D)
Thank you for your time, gentlemen.

He steps away from reporters with his mug in a bunch.

EXT. ILLINOIS – DAY

Alice appears MUCH skinner since the last time we saw her. She walks from house to house handing out fliers for a women's convention. Another woman is across the street doing the same thing.

EXT. NEVADA – DAY

Inez is worse off than Alice as she marches door to door with her fliers. She's skinnier, weaker, and looks as though she hasn't slept in weeks.

EXT. ARIZONA – DAY

Lucy doesn't give the impression that she's as bad off as Alice and

Inez, but she does come across as being extremely exhausted as she hands out fliers door to door.

                INEZ (V.O.)
Patience might be a virtue at home. In the political arena, however, it means defeat.

EXT. NEVADA – DAY

Inez's breathing sounds very weak as she speaks. Her legs shake, knees wobble.
                    INEZ
Whether we succeed in defeating President Wilson is of secondary importance.
              (swaying/steadying herself)
What we must do is show him and every other political leader that women are ready to revolt against hostility.

And with that, Inez no longer has the strength to steady herself. She crumbles. People scream. Women rush to her side. One man fans her. Inez regains consciousness after several seconds.

                  WOMAN
Drink some water, Inez.

She takes a sip of water.
                          INEZ
          I need to finish my speech.

                          MAN
          No, no, you must rest.

                          INEZ
          No, I was almost done.

People glance at each other. Nobody knows what to do. Inez seems too firmly set on finishing.

                        WOMAN
          Get her a chair. If she wants to finish her speech, she'll have to do it sitting.
                        (to Inez)
          And I won't have you telling me different.
                        (chokes up)
          You're really giving this everything you've got, aren't you, dear?

They grin at each other. Several people stand her up only to sit her down.
                          INEZ
          Thank you.
                        (to crowd)
          You'll have to excuse me. I get excited at the thought of revolting.

The crowd laughs.
                        INEZ (V.O.)
          I think my fight spurred people on. You should have seen them, Alice. They were crying.

INT. HOSPITAL – NIGHT

Inez is in a hospital bed fighting for her life. Alice is in her own fight not to break down crying. She's holding Inez's hand. Also in the room is VIDA MILHOLLAND, Lucy, and Dora.

> INEZ
> I got us a lot of publicity, didn't I?

Alice nods but can't smile. Lucy snatches up a newspaper.

> ALICE
> You did. The *world* is up in arms now.

> LUCY
> Check this out: "Never before, except among a few enthusiasts, had there existed any feeling suffrage was a thing to fight for, suffer for, even to die for."

> DORA
> Lucy!

> LUCY
> What? She's not gonna *die*.

> INEZ
> No. That was lovely. It was the best quote I've ever heard about myself.
> (narrows her eyes)
> Have you ladies been holding back all the exciting quotes about me?

Alice smiles and this cracks the dam in her eyes.

> ALICE
> I'm sorry, Inez. I shouldn't have pushed you so hard.

Dora rushes to Alice's side to console her, as does Lucy.

DORA
Shhh. Stop that, honey. Please don't do this to yourself.

Inez hasn't spoken with a lot of energy throughout this scene, but she now squeezes Alice's hand and there's a fire in her eyes, though the rest of her is in a weakened state. She sits up on an elbow. Feeling her hand being squeezed, Alice glances up.

INEZ
If I die from this, you better not show any weakness. You *have* to capitalize off of it by blaming my death on the men who made us fight this way.

She flops back down on the bed. She closes her eyes for a second, exhausted by the short passionate moment.

VIDA
If there's one thing I know about my sister, it's that she wouldn't want her death to be in vain.

DORA
Even if Hughes doesn't beat Wilson tonight, he at least won Arizona. Shows your efforts won the state.

LUCY
And Jeannette Rankin won, too. We got our first woman in Congress.

Inez forces a smile before falling asleep. Dora rubs her hand.

DORA
Let's give Vida some time alone with her sister.

VIDA
Thanks.

They exit the room. Alice is the last to leave. She appears as though she has so much more to say. They walk into a waiting room where nurses and doctors are gathered around a radio listening to the presidential election results.

Alice and the other two sit. Nobody says anything to each other. Lucy closes her eyes. Dora and Alice stare at nothing.

INT. HOSPITAL – MORNING

Alice, Dora, and Lucy are sleeping in the waiting room. Only a DOCTOR remains listening to the radio.

> DOCTOR
>
> Yes!

Alice awakes. The doctor sees he woke her up, but he doesn't care. He grins at her.

> DOCTOR (CONT'D)
>
> Wilson won.

This wakes up Lucy and Dora. Vida is not in the waiting room, though. She's in the hall speaking with a doctor. She covers her face and sobs. Alice observes this.

> ALICE
>
> Oh no.

Alice stands. Vida walks over to the trio. She can't speak. She breaks down. Alice walks over and embraces her. Lucy and Dora see this and do the same thing. They all weep for Inez, a fallen sister.

EXT. HOSPITAL – DAY

Alice walks out of the hospital wiping tears away. This isn't the time for weakness, and Alice refuses to show any. Dora and Lucy pick up on the pep in her step and quicken theirs.

LUCY
What do we do now?

ALICE
We hold a press conference. Immediately. Wilson can have
the headlines today... But we'll own them tomorrow.

EXT. NWP HEADQUARTERS – DAY

Alice stands beside Vida holding a cross with Jesus on it. Many
women stand behind them. REPORTERS and PHOTOGRAPHERS
huddle up in a large group to hear, write, and take photos. Vida
holds up a photograph of Inez.

ALICE
As he died to make men holy, let us die to make men free.

VIDA
How much longer must women suffer for freedom, Mr.
President?

Vida can barely get that out. Whatever strength she had shatters
and she weeps for her sister. Women console her. Even some of
the reporters and photographers choke up.

EXT. STREET CORNER – DAY

A BOY holds a newspaper in his hands and shouts for all to hear.

BOY
Mrs. Milholland dies for suffrage! Read all about it! Wilson
celebrates while a nation mourns!

People toss coins to the boy and snatch up the newspapers. Other
people walk from another street corner while reading a different
newspaper that reads, "WILL THE PRESIDENT DO ANYTHING
NOW?"

EXT. U.S. CAPITOL – DAY

Women march into the Capitol by the hundreds. They're exactly one thousand strong.

INT. U.S. CAPITOL – ROTUNDA – DAY

Alice has truly created a martyr out of Inez Milholland. Christmas decorations and photos of Inez are all over the rotunda. She's made her a Christ-like figure.

> ALICE
> We're gathered here on Christmas Day to celebrate the memory of Inez Milholland: daughter, wife, sister, friend, suffragist, and so much more.

Alice, looking worse since the last time we saw her, turns to Inez's husband, mother, father, sister, and other family members.

> ALICE (CONT'D)
> A thousand people have rearranged their holiday schedules to commemorate this amazing woman and what she stood for, and we pray our government has recognized the greatness of the cause she fought for. . . Our president has been silent about the tragedy that has befallen our sister, and we at the National Woman's Party have decided to match his weapon of silence with one of our own, which will begin next year. All in the name of Inez Milholland.

The crowd cheers. Inez's family nod their heads in thanks to Alice. Vida mouths "thank you" and places a hand over her heart.

INT. NWP HEADQUARTERS – DAY

Alice and the gang arrive back from celebrating Inez's life and sacrifice at the Capitol. Alice goes straight to her room. As soon as her bedroom door shuts, she drops her jacket and other items in her hands and sobs.

She's headed for her bed, but she's racked with body shaking cries and falls to her knees in front of it. She screams into the mattress so that nobody can hear her.

When silence overcomes the room, she can hear Dora in the next room on the phone.

                    DORA (O.S.)
          I know I've been away from home for a long time, but... I
          know. I miss you, too, my beloved husband, but because
          Jessica's sick, I'll be home shortly...

Alice wraps a pillow around her head so that she doesn't have to hear the conversation any longer.

Her bedroom door opens. Its Dora. She rushes to her side.

                    DORA (CONT'D)
          Oh dear.

Alice pulls herself together and sits on her bed wiping tears away. Her wall of strength back up.

                    ALICE
          I'm fine, just needed a good cry.

                    DORA
          I came in here to tell you that I have a sister who is sick and
          I need to watch over her for a while, but I can't leave you
          like this.

Alice appears as if she weren't crying mere seconds ago. She eyes Dora like she is being ridiculous.

                    ALICE
          Stop it. I'm fine. You should also take time for yourself.
          You've been constantly watching over me and others.
          Focus your energies inward for a change.

Dora gauges her.

                         DORA
     I may do that, but you have to take care of yourself while
     I'm away.

Alice grins, trying to project confidence into Dora about her next
words.

                         ALICE
     For you, Dora, I will.

EXT. NWP HEADQUARTERS – DAY

Alice and eleven other women step out of the house bearing
banners that read, "Mr. President, what will you do for woman
suffrage?" and "How many more women must die for liberty?"

They march all the way to the White House. Alice doesn't lead the
way. She's moving very slowly. This is the worst she's ever
appeared. She stops, takes out a necklace, and falls to one knee.
She kisses the crucifix.

                         ALICE
     Lord, please give me strength.

Alice seems to know exactly where this road leads, and the worry
lines on her forehead, how she can barely rise off the ground, and
her lethargic manner as she picks up the pace to catch up with the
other suffragists shows how she doesn't think she'll make it to the
end.

EXT. WHITE HOUSE – DAY

Alice and the women silently picket in front of the White House.
Some people walk by laughing. Some cheer them on. Some mock
them. Some shout curses at them, but, still, the women remain
silent.

One man with a red flower in his fedora spits on the ground at the
women. We'll call him FLOWER HAT MAN.

FLOWER HAT MAN
Disgraceful!! Picketing the White House? Where's your patriotism?

He shakes his head and walks away. Time passes. Even though the women are bundled up with heavy coats and gloves, they're tortured souls from the freezing cold. REPORTERS arrive to question them.

REPORTER
Is this the protest in honor of Inez Milholland?

JOURNALIST
How long do you plan on doing this for?

REPORTER
Don't you think there are lines you're crossing by behaving this way toward our nation's president?

Twelve other women arrive. They take up banners and replace Alice and the eleven women. Alice, now off of silent sentinel duty, turns to the reporter, her teeth chattering and body shivering.

ALICE
Has the president crossed any lines by allowing women to die for freedom? He can stop our suffering at any time.

She walks away.

INT. NWP HEADQUARTERS – DAY

Alice now appears as bad as Inez did before she died. She's flipping through letters, scanning them. She slaps them on the table. Lucy walks into the room and sees them.

LUCY
What's wrong?

Alice loses her breath as she talks, but she does not lack for passion, which makes her seem almost normal.

> ALICE
> It feels like NOBODY is supporting us on our silent picketing. Even other suffrage organizations are asking for us to stop.

Greta Graham, now a suffragist, steps into the room.

> GRETA
> I'm sorry to interrupt, Alice, but when you get a chance, can I speak to you in private, please?

> ALICE
> You want to leave due to the picketing?

Greta nods. Her head falls as she does so.

> GRETA
> It just doesn't feel right.

> ALICE
> It's okay, Greta. You're entitled to your opinion. Please see Sarah and let her know.

Greta nods, and as she leaves the room, Alice gestures at her while looking at Lucy like, "SEE!"

> LUCY
> For every woman who leaves, another fifty join us. We have nothing to worry about.

EXT. NWP HEADQUARTERS – DAY

Greta exits the house only to see suffragists braving the cold and lining down the street to enter NWP headquarters. A YOUNG SUFFRAGIST stops Greta from leaving.

YOUNG SUFFRAGIST
This is the line to sign up to picket the White House, right?

GRETA
Yes.

She walks off only to hear all these women she's passing are praising Alice and her new strategy.

ADMIRER #1
What a bold move by Alice.

ADMIRER #2
We're going to be making history by participating in this!

ADMIRER #3
We'll be the first people to ever picket the White House.

ADMIRER #4
Because you *know* others will copy Alice in the future!

ADMIRER #3
Yeah, like the NAWSA.

INT. NWP HEADQUARTERS – DAY

Alice is speaking with Lucy and a couple other women when Greta enters. Her presence silences Alice. She waits for Greta to speak.

GRETA
I've changed my mind. Can I come back?

ALICE
Of course you can.

Alice approaches her. Greta smiles, but her face is red with shame. Alice reaches out and picks her chin up.

ALICE (CONT'D)
What we're searching for in all this isn't to hurt anybody, Greta. It's headlines. Publicity results immediately in discussion, and discussion is the essence of politics.

LUCY
Ohhh, that's good. We gotta get that in our next issue of *The Suffragist*.

A SUFFRAGETTE races into the room. All turn to her.

SUFFRAGETTE
We're going to war. They're announcing it over the radio now.

The women rush over to the radio and listen.

RADIO
So it is official. After four days of Congress debating the war resolution, the decision is for us to enter the European war.

SUFFRAGETTE
Wilson was said to have made the comment, "The world must be made safe for democracy." I can't remember the rest.

Another NWP MEMBER grabs a notepad.

NWP MEMBER
I wrote it down. He's talking about democracy here: "The right is more precious than peace, and we shall fight for the things we have always carried nearest to our hearts."

LUCY
That lying bastard.

SUFFRAGETTE
What do we do now? We can't possibly go on picketing when we're going to war.

NWP MEMBER
It certainly doesn't feel right.

ALICE
Susan B. Anthony was told to stop pressuring the government when we went to war and that consideration of woman suffrage would be held after the war ended. And we all know how that worked out for her.

Alice pauses to eye all the women in the room.

ALICE (CONT'D)
This war is about democracy, supposedly. If that's true, we, as Americans, should receive it before fighting for other nations' freedom.

LUCY
All of this needs to be in the next *Suffragist* issue.

ALICE
What also must happen is for us to spread these truths to every reporter, get it printed in every newspaper. Expose the hypocrisy. Democracy *MUST* begin at home.

EXT. WASHINGTON D.C. – DAY

Alice struggles to walk with eleven other women to the White House. A couple women of color walk with her. One is MARY CHURCH TERELL. She holds up a banner that reads, "The National Association of Colored Women's Clubs is with Alice."

Alice and another woman carry the biggest banner seen yet. It says, "Dear Russia, President Wilson is deceiving you by saying we are all a democracy. 'Help us win a world war so that democracies may survive,' he says. We, the women of America, tell you that America is not a democracy. President Wilson is the chief opponent of women's national enfranchisement. Tell our government that it must liberate its people before it can claim free Russia as an ally."

Because they're not in front of the White House yet to silently picket, Mary speaks to Alice.

MARY
Not even afraid to have me along in the segregated Jim Crow South. You truly are one remarkable woman, Alice.

ALICE
Having Mary Church Terell's name attached to mine is my honor; I promise you.

MARY
This is so dangerous for me, you, and for your entire organization. I can only see myself doing this once with you, my dear.

Alice nods her understanding. They've made it to the White House and can no longer speak. People see this banner and shake their heads in disgust. Flower Hat Man glares at them.

FLOWER HAT MAN
I should rip that banner down. You women have no class.

A REPORTER walks over to Alice with the whites of his eyes showing.
REPORTER
Are you going to show this to the Russian envoys arriving today? I know you're silent sentinels, but you can nod your head if I'm right.

Alice nods. The reporter scribbles furiously into his notepad while reading the banner.

Time passes.

The Russian envoys arrive at the White House. The reporter quickly gets his notepad and pencil ready. Alice and another woman place the banner in such a way so that is can be read with ease.

One of the vehicles stops. A RUSSIAN takes the time to read the message and then drives on. The reporter writes all of this down. From one of the White House windows, the president eyes the pickets with hate.

INT. WHITE HOUSE – DAY

President Wilson glares at the pickets as the Russian envoy exits White House grounds. Inside the room with him is DUDLEY MALONE and POLICE COMMISSIONER BROWNLOW.

> PRESIDENT
> I want these pickets jailed, Commissioner Brownlow.

Dudley Malone's and Commissioner Brownlow's eyes widen.

> COMMISSIONER
> For what?

President Wilson spins on him.

> PRESIDENT
> I don't know! Obstructing traffic. I don't care, just make it happen.

> COMMISSIONER
> But... most people don't go to jail for obstructing traffic, especially if it's their first offense.

President's eyes narrow at the commissioner.

> COMMISSIONER (CONT'D)
> I'll have to speak with the district judges to make — —

PRESIDENT

— — If you want, you can tell them the president himself has ordered this unpatriotic nonsense to come to an end. Three days in jail should be good enough to teach them a lesson.

DUDLEY

Mr. President, are you sure you don't want to sleep on this?

PRESIDENT

Before I even slept in the White House, these women were at my doorstep. I've slept long enough, thank you very much.

Dudley eyes the floor with uncertainty.

INT. NWP HEADQUARTERS – DAY

Alice is writing when Lucy knocks and immediately enters her room. Alice doesn't even stop writing.

LUCY

I have to talk to you about something important.

Alice sets her pen down, turns to Lucy, and gives her her undivided attention.

LUCY (CONT'D)

Alice, I've met someone. I really like him, and we've been at this for *years* now... so — —

Alice's body slumps and sags. In an instant, Alice appears to have aged decades.

ALICE

— — You want to quit.

LUCY

No! I just don't think I can dedicate so much time to this anymore.

Alice eyes the floor.

                    LUCY (CONT'D)
I want a family, Alice. I want to be a mom.

                      ALICE
I need your fire, Lucy. Without it... my flame will die out.

Lucy smiles and rushes over to Alice. She grabs her hands.

                      LUCY
Nobody could ever extinguish the volcano that's inside
you, girl.
                      ALICE
Please hold on, just for a bit longer. I mean, Inez is gone,
Dora just left, and now *you're* leaving, too? At least wait
until Dora comes back.

Lucy sadly grins and squeezes her hands tighter.

                      LUCY
I can do that.

INT. NWP HEADQUARTERS – DAY

Dora walks into the house with her eyes wide and mouth tight.
Lucy freezes upon seeing her, knowing something's up.

                      LUCY
I would say welcome back, but I can tell something's
wrong.
                      DORA
The pickets have been arrested. Where's Alice?

                      LUCY
In her room.

Dora rushes to Alice's room. She opens the door without
knocking. Alice is changing into a dress. Dora is knocked back by

an invisible blow. It's Alice's unnaturally skinny frame, bones protruding everywhere, a living skeleton.

In a very lifeless and listless way, Alice's head turns to see Dora's frightened countenance. Alice passes out. Dora screams and runs to her side.

INT. JOHNS HOPKINS HOSPITAL – DAY

Alice is in a hospital bed unconscious. Dora is sitting by her side holding her hand. Flowers are everywhere. Greta enters the room. When Dora sees her, her heart sinks.

        DORA
Where's Lucy?

        GRETA
Jail.

        DORA
Oh, god, help us.

        GRETA
Have the doctors said anything?

Dora bites her bottom lip and summons an other-worldly strength.

        DORA
They say she'll probably make it, but she'll have to remain in the hospital for a couple weeks thereafter. But, Greta, that's exactly what they said about Inez. And she could actually speak! Alice has just been *unconscious*.

Dora can no longer hold back the tears. Greta's nostrils flare as she sucks in as much fortitude as Alice used to carry.

                          GRETA
We need her wisdom. She would know exactly what to do
right now.
                          ALICE
                      (barely audible)
Keep fighting.

                          DORA
Alice? Alice! What did you say, darling?

Alice's eyelids flutter open.

                          ALICE
The only wisdom I have is to keep fighting.

Each word she speaks shows a rise in her strength. It even gives
hope to Dora. She can't help but crack a smile at Alice's
indomitable spirit.
                          DORA
How do you fee — —

                          ALICE
— — What are they being charged with?

                          GRETA
Obstructing traffic.

Alice looks confused.

                          DORA
Nothing's different. Nobody's in the streets or anything.
What happens is police officers demand the pickets to
surrender their banners. The women refuse and they are
promptly arrested.

                          ALICE
How are the conditions in jail?

GRETA
Lucy said there's some good and some bad, but it's mostly better than England and Scotland.

Alice nods and releases the breath she was holding. We can see those wheels turning in Alice's head through those determined eyes of hers. Dora grabs her hand again.

DORA
You almost worked yourself to death. I'm scared of you ending up like...

She can't say Inez's name. Alice squeezes her hand.

ALICE
I won't... Listen, I know my obsession with winning the vote may seem like a flaw to you, but we NEED this. I'm not purposely forgetting to eat and sleep, you know.

DORA
I know. But now you're going to be here for two weeks.

Alice swats those words away.

ALICE
This IS something to die for, but I'm not ready to go. And I'll tell you, Wilson's going to wish that were my outcome when I get out of here.

Alice's fight bleeds through her mien.

INT. WHITE HOUSE – DAY

President Wilson is sitting across from Police Commissioner Brownlow in the Oval Office. Dudley sits beside the president.

PRESIDENT
Why do I care if the jail is overflowing with these crazy women?

DUDLEY
Because it appears as if you don't care, Mr. President.
Politically, it hurts the entire party.

COMMISSIONER
We can begin filling the jails in Virginia, but it will take
resources.

PRESIDENT
I don't mind spending the money to get these demons off
our lawn.

Dudley shakes his head. President Wilson turns on him.

PRESIDENT (CONT'D)
Have something you want to say, Dudley?

DUDLEY
Yes, thirty-six pickets have been jailed so far. Twelve a day!
They don't care about jail time. They want the vote.

PRESIDENT
They'll run out of bodies to throw at us.

DUDLEY
Bodies? Is that how you think of them?

PRESIDENT
You're behaving as irrationally as these women. Come
now. No need to get all emotional.

Dudley seethes while President Wilson is considering something.

PRESIDENT (CONT'D)
You know, Dudley, you do make a good point.
Commissioner, talk to the judges. We need to
Increase their jail time.

COMMISSIONER
To what, Mr. President?

Wilson grins.

INT. CAR – DAY

A WOMAN CHAUFFEUR drives a healthier Alice and Dora to NWP headquarters. A rowdy mob is outside of it. Lucy steps out of the door with a banner that causes the mob to erupt. One of the men is Flower Hat Man.

The banner reads, "Kaiser Wilson, have you forgotten your sympathy with the poor Germans because they were not self-governed? 20,000,000 American women are not self-governed. Take the beam out of your own eye."

Flower Hat Man and others rip the banners from Lucy and the twelve suffragists. Three men snatch up Lucy and drag her into the street.

Alice closes her eyes and sucks in three calming breaths while opening the car door. Her eyes blaze open and she's transformed from a weak hospitalized patient into a Warrior for Justice.

EXT. NWP HEADQUARTERS – CONTINUOUS

Alice jumps out of the car. The mob is roughing up all the women, but she fearlessly pushes one man after another off of them. One man punches her hard to the ground. She bumps her head. Darkness.

INT. WHITE HOUSE – DAY

President Wilson is sitting behind a desk reading documents when Dudley Malone enters the room. He has some documents of his own. Wilson waves him over. Dudley sets his resignation down on the president's desk, along with data.

PRESIDENT
What can I do for you, Dudley?

DUDLEY
I'm offering you my resignation. I intend to serve as the suffragists' council, and I don't believe it right to represent them while working under the administration responsible for subjecting these same women to *sixty days of jail time* for obstructing traffic.

As Dudley speaks, the president's worry lines in his forehead deepen. He senses a scandal brewing, but he composes himself quickly and flips through the data to collect his thoughts.

PRESIDENT
What are these other papers?

DUDLEY
It's data showing that if you put your weight behind the Anthony Amendment it would easily pass both houses.

The president scans the information and sets it down. He eyes Dudley.
PRESIDENT
I will have a cabinet member go over this for verification.
(purses lips)
But I won't accept your resignation. I will pardon these women and order Commissioner Brownlow to stop arresting them.

Dudley's tense shoulders relax. He looks upon the president with gratitude.
DUDLEY
Thank you, Mr. President.

The president's nod and countenance are dismissive. Without another word, Dudley bows and exits.

INT. NWP HEADQUARTERS – DAY

Dora is mothering Alice by trying to check the injury to her head as Alice hustles around to put together another KAISER WILSON banner. Dora presses a cloth against Alice's head.

> DORA
> The wound is still bleeding, Alice. You *can't* go out and picket.

She shows Alice the cloth for proof. There's not that much blood at all.

> ALICE
> It's only a couple of small specks.

She goes back to work on the banner. It's just about finished. Lucy is smiling ear to ear. She LOVES the fight. Alice notices the wide grin and smiles broadly, too. They laugh excitedly.

> LUCY
> It's like we're back in England!

They laugh some more. These women are implacable soldiers, and the other ladies in the room gawk at them in admiration, many of them bandaged up from the angry mob and not smiling like them. One of them is Greta.

> LUCY (CONT'D)
> They're not going to let us get to the White House with these banners. We've been trying for *days* now.
> (teasing)
> While you've been resting in bed for *weeks*.

> DORA
> In a *hospital*! You're not healthy enough to go to jail, Alice.

> GRETA
> You're not going to go on a hunger strike when you get there, are you?

Alice grins.

> ALICE
>
> Do I seem as though I have a death wish?

> DORA
>
> You didn't answer her question!

Dora's explosive outburst stops everybody in the room from gazing on Alice and Lucy with worshipful eyes. They all turn to Dora. Alice regains control of her excitement for a fight and hugs Dora.

> ALICE
>
> I love you. I love who you are.

She continues to embrace Dora tenderly.

> ALICE (CONT'D)
>
> I'm sorry my behavior's frightened you. I do NOT plan to go on a hunger strike.

Dora's muscles loosen up on hearing this. Alice holds her to arm's length.

> ALICE (CONT'D)
>
> I plan on working while I'm back there.

> DORA
>
> Isn't there another way?

Alice stares deeply into Dora's eyes.

> ALICE
>
> No. The time has come to conquer or submit. For me, there can be but one choice.

Dora's head falls. Alice releases her, snatches up her finished KAISER WILSON banner, and turns to the rest of the women. They're now standing there holding banners, ready to follow her through hell if they have to.

ALICE (CONT'D)
We will go out the back door this time.

The freedom fighters depart with their heads held high and victory in their eyes.

EXT. WHITE HOUSE – DAY

Alice, Lucy, and the rest of the crew arrive at the White House gates. Police arrive, and they stand around *protecting* the women from a mob of people who gather.

The pickets are supposed to be silent sentinels, so Alice can only throw a look at Lucy that says, "Why aren't they arresting us?" Lucy shrugs. The mob grows in its size and hostility. A red flower in a fedora stands out in the crowd.

Flower Hat Man breaks through the line of officers and strips Alice of her banner. Other men break the line. The officers can't control the crowd. The men rough up the women and destroy the banners.

INT. POLICE DEPARTMENT – DAY

Police Commissioner Brownlow is on the phone and is passionately pleading his case.

COMMISSIONER
Mr. President, every day *for a week* riots have been caused by the suffragists. Ever since we stopped incarcerating these women, the public has come to view them as miscreants. They're having no more of their nonsense.

INT. WHITE HOUSE – CONTINUOUS

The president breathes heavily. The worry lines in his forehead are as deep as ever.
PRESIDENT
What do you expect me to do, Commissioner Brownlow?

INTERCUT – PHONE CONVERSATION

                         COMMISSIONER
Untie me! We need to take action! Maybe before we didn't,
but now we certainly do.

President Wilson's breathing quickens.

                         PRESIDENT
We need to talk to the press about these *belligerent* pickets
and their *riotous behavior* before we do anything. Do you
follow me?
                         COMMISSIONER
Yes, sir.
                         PRESIDENT
But you're taking full responsibility.

                         COMMISSIONER
I will, sir.

                         PRESIDENT
And, Commissioner?

                         COMMISSIONER
Yes, sir?

                         PRESIDENT
I want their jail time increased again.

INT. NWP HEADQUARTERS – DAY

Alice, Lucy, and other women are busy writing letters, creating
banners, or initiating new women into the NWP. Dudley Malone
is escorted to where Alice is. He knocks on the open door.

                         DUDLEY
Helloooo? Is Alice Paul here?

Alice raises her head.

ALICE

Yes, sir.

She stands and walks over to him. They shake hands.

DUDLEY

Hi, I'm Dudley Malone.

Recognition shows clearly on her face on hearing his name. Alice gestures for him to follow her.

ALICE

Shall we step into my office?

DUDLEY

It appears as though everywhere is your office.

He says this as they step into a corner of a hallway. She smiles. There are a couple chairs there, though. They take a seat.

ALICE

So, how can I help you?

DUDLEY

I just resigned from President Wilson's administration, and I want to represent you in court.

Alice focuses on him and nods.

ALICE

This is a historic moment for the movement. But... I sense that you have more for me.

From his expression, we know this is true.

INT. COURTROOM – DAY

Dudley is legally defending the group of women in court. Many reporters and photographers pack the courthouse. Photographers snap photos of Dudley and the women. Alice is in the audience watching. The JUDGE is wrapping up.

> JUDGE
> You women are causing all sorts of trouble, and I don't see much else to do but to continue increasing your sentences until you all understand this behavior won't be tolerated.
> (sighs)
> That being said, I sentence each of you to six months in prison.

A buzz enters the courtroom.

EXT. COURT HOUSE – DAY

Dudley and Alice are hounded by questions from reporters as they exit the court house.

> REPORTER
> Alice, how do you feel about Dudley Malone leaving the president's administration to join the National Woman's Party?
> ALICE
> I'm honored, first off, but it's also the first outward sign of doubt and disillusion within the president's own inner circle.
> REPORTER
> Mr. Malone, is there anything you'd like to say about the status quo?
> DUDLEY
> I *say* it is high time that something besides cheap politics be demanded from our government.

> ALICE

This victory for democracy could be accomplished without struggle, without grief, without... the loss of a single life.

These words hit reporters. They bow their heads to write them down.

INT. NWP HEADQUARTERS – DAY

Alice is all bundled up in a thick fur coat. Dora secures it, looking her directly in the eyes. Dora's eyes are on the verge of dripping tears.

> DORA

Please take care of yourself, honey.

> ALICE

I will.

> DORA

Tell Lucy I said I love her.

Alice nods and hugs her.

> DORA (CONT'D)

And I love you, too.

> ALICE

I love you, Dora.

Dudley is waiting over by the door. Dora and Alice separate. She walks over to him and hugs him, too.

> DUDLEY

I'll pay you a visit every Friday to discuss work.

> ALICE

Sounds good.

Alice grabs her weapon of choice: it's a banner that reads, "Mr. President, what will you do for woman suffrage?" She takes one last look at Dudley and Dora and all the other women. She smiles before heading out the door.

EXT. WHITE HOUSE – DAY

Twelve women march to the front of the White House gates. All of them are wearing purple, white, and gold.

A mob of people almost immediately attacks them and tears down their banners. Of course, Flower Hat Man is among them.

They stand there silently awaiting the police. Alice holds a bare staff. The police show up and arrest them. They lead the women into a patrol wagon and drive away.

INT. COURTROOM – DAY

SUPER:			October 22nd, 1917

The courtroom is PACKED. Dudley is there to lend his legal aid to the women. It's the same judge as before.

> JUDGE
> Counsel, how do your clients plead?

Right when Dudley opens his mouth, Alice speaks up for the group.
> ALICE
> We do not consider ourselves subject to this court since, as an unenfranchised class, we have nothing to do with the making of the laws.
> JUDGE
> (to the other women)
> All of you feel the same way?
> (they nod)

Well, I guess we'll move to sentencing since I find you all guilty.

He moves papers around on his desk.

JUDGE (CONT'D)
I sentence all the defendants, apart from Miss Paul, to 6 months in jail. Seeing as though Miss Alice Paul is the ringleader of this movement, I am forced to take the most drastic means in my power to compel her to obey the law. I sentence Miss Paul to seven months in prison.

He bangs the gavel, and that's that. Alice and the group are led through the court by officers. Reporters scramble to ask questions. One side steps beside her as she's being escorted away.

REPORTER
Alice, what are you thinking right now?

ALICE
I think I am being imprisoned not because I obstructed traffic but because I pointed out the fact that President Wilson is obstructing the progress of democracy and justice at home, while Americans fight for it abroad.

Alice sees her mother in the crowd. Mrs. Paul appears terribly worried. Alice turns to an officer.

ALICE (CONT'D)
Please let me say goodbye to my mother.

The officer takes pity on her and stops. Mrs. Paul hurries over and hugs her daughter. Alice's countenance reveals that she just knows her mom's going to say how worried she is.

MRS. PAUL
I had to tell thee that I've never been prouder. Thee has *me* believing we can see a world where women are equal to men and hold the same respect. Thy bravery is admired.

ALICE
Thank you, Mother.

Alice's shock and affection make her eyes water. They part, and she and the group of women leave the court house.

EXT. DISTRICT JAIL – DAY

The suffragists exit a patrol wagon and enter the jail.

INT. DISTRICT JAIL – DAY

Inside, the air is dusty. Each suffragist is loaded down with a blanket, sheets, and a care package that has a toothbrush, soap, etc. As they make their way to their cells, big rats scurry along beside them, completely unafraid.

Some of the ladies scream. Alice doesn't. None of this appears new to her. They make it to their cells.

A GUARD waves a hand for Alice to enter a small dusty cell that has one bed, one sink, and one toilet. Lucy is in there. Alice doesn't realize there's only one bed. She has eyes only for Lucy. Lucy sits up.
LUCY
Well, look who decided to finally jump into the spotlight.

The guard closes the door and locks them in. They hug. Alice holds her to arm's length.

ALICE
Oh, it is good to see you. You look healthy.

LUCY
I am fat and flourishing.

They laugh. Alice notices something on her shirt.

ALICE

What is this?

She goes to remove the little black thing off Lucy's shirt until it moves.

LUCY

Oh, that is a bed bug. They're everywhere. Look.

She lifts up a blanket and the sheet underneath, and it is nearly black from all the bed bugs.

ALICE

I don't remember them being this bad in England.

LUCY

(smiling)

Just wait till you see the food.

ALICE

Wait, there's only one bed?

LUCY

They are filled to capacity because of us.

(eyes her seductively)

We get to share a bed now.

Loud banging noises come from outside the cell.

LUCY (CONT'D)

That's chow.

Lucy smiles so broadly it raises Alice's eyebrows. She knows this food must be something terrible. The banging gets closer. The door opens. They're each handed a tray. The pork they are served is crawling with maggots. Alice's upper lip curls. Lucy laughs.

LUCY (CONT'D)

Much worse than England, right?

Lucy laughs some more at Alice's reaction.

                    LUCY (CONT'D)
Look.
                (brushes away maggots)
All you have to do is shut your eyes tight, close your mouth
over it, and swallow it without chewing.

Lucy demonstrates. Alice is absolutely horrified. She gags. Alice
wipes the maggots off and tears herself a swallowable bite. She
takes several deep breaths of the dusty air.

                      ALICE
The air doesn't help at all.

                    PRISONER (O.S.)
                (singsong)
Shoulder to shoulder, friend to friend.

                      LUCY
Oh, yeah, we always sing a song for this meal since it's the
worst.

Lucy and the other inmates sing.

                  LUCY/PRISONERS
We worried woody-wood.
As we stood, as we stood.
We asked for some air,
And they threw us in the lair.
Now ladies take the hint.
Don't quote the president.
Don't quote the president.

They repeat this three times. The unity between the women
brings tears to Alice's eyes.

INT. DISTRICT JAIL – DAY

Alice and Lucy are lying in bed. They're sharing a newspaper.

Alice holds one side. Lucy holds the other. A GUARD comes around and unlocks all the doors.

                         GUARD
    Rec. time.

Lucy and Alice step out of their cell. Alice hugs all of her sisters-in-arms.

                         ALICE
    Hello, ladies. How are you holding up?

                        FRIENDS
    We have no regrets.

Alice nods.

                         ALICE
    Well, I have no intention in staying here seven months.

She grins, takes off a shoe, and busts out a window. And another window. And another. The women are shocked at first. Then they laugh, cheer, and stick their faces out the windows to take in some fresh air.

Lucy breaks some windows with her. GUARD #1 only catches Alice breaking windows and stomps over to her.

                        GUARD #1
    What do you think you are doing?

Alice inhales deeply out a window. She eyes Guard #1.

                         ALICE
                    (very dignified)
    Getting some fresh air. It's stifling in here.

He snatches her up. She grabs on to one of the bars barring the window with both hands. She clings to it with everything she has. GUARD #2 enters the pod and comes to Guard #1's rescue.

Alice lets out a battle cry as both guards pull on her. Inmates cheer her on. They yank her off, and all three of them fall to the floor. The guards stand and drag Alice to her cell. Women shout at them.

> WOMAN #1
>
> Let her up!

> WOMAN #2
>
> Don't drag her, you bastards!

> WOMAN#3
>
> Y'all aren't men!

The guards throw her in a cell and Guard #1 slaps her around. The slapping disturbs Guard #2. Guard #1 mushes her face into the floor. He pushes his nose against her ear.

> GUARD #1
>
> You're *nothing* in here, bitch.
> (to Guard #2)
> Hold her down.

Guard #1 rises and Guard #2 hesitantly pins her to the floor. Guard #1 slides his boot up to her mouth.

> GUARD #1 (CONT'D)
>
> Kiss it.

Alice's lips pucker. She spits on his shoe. The saliva is mixed with blood. Blood is also running out of her nose. Guard #1 raises his boot ready to stomp her face in. Guard #2 pushes his foot away.

> GUARD #2
>
> We can't do that. Not to her, anyway. Slapping her is one thing, but if we *really* hurt her, we're in some trouble.

Guard #1 glares at her. Guard #2 stands and pulls the other guard out of there. Before shutting the door, he glances at Alice sympathetically. Alice goes to the sink and cleans herself up.

The door opens and Lucy enters. The door clinks shut and is locked behind her.

>   LUCY
> You're not going to be able to come out the cell for ten days.

>   ALICE
> I don't think I can survive another hunger strike.

>   LUCY
> We don't need to do it. We have influence now. The NWP is lobbying to Congress for our release as I speak these words to you.

>   ALICE
> I'm not eating that meat.

>   LUCY
> They serve it nearly every day so that will be a problem for you. They also stopped allowing us to order food off canteen since you got arrested. It will be a rough road for you if you don't eat it.

Alice gets her head out of the sink, dries her face, and grabs a piece of paper and a writing utensil.

>   ALICE
> I am going to paint the most disturbing image of this place for newspapers.

>   LUCY
> You can't send out letters or receive mail or visitors when you're on solitary confinement status.

She continues to write.

>   ALICE
> One of the other ladies here can send this out for me.

> LUCY
They are already doing all they can, Alice.

Alice doesn't care. She's SUPER fired up as she writes.

INT. DISTRICT JAIL – DAY

SUPER: 10 DAYS LATER

Alice is in rough shape: She's skinny as hell. She has dark circles around her eyes. She's sucked up. The door of her cell opens. Lucy sits up. Alice continues to lie there.

> GUARD #1
Let's go, Miss Paul.

> LUCY
Where are you taking her?

> GUARD #1
To the ward. Look at her. She might die. We've all noticed. And *somehow* your friends on the street know, too. All right, upsy daisy.

He bangs a flashlight against the door. Alice rises like she's an old woman. Guard #1 laughs at his rushing her.

> GUARD #1 (CONT'D)
Come on, Miss Snail's Pace.

INT. DISTRICT JAIL – WARD – DAY

Guard #1 assists Alice to a table where there's a big glass of milk and large bowl of steaming scrambled eggs. A NURSE awaits her there.

> ALICE
What is this?

> NURSE
> (to Guard #1)
> I'll take it from here. Thanks.

Guard #1 tips his hat to the nurse and walks away.

> ALICE
> If this is for me, I'm not going to eat it.

> NURSE
> I certainly hope you will. Look at you! We don't want you dying on us.

> ALICE
> I will only eat if it's provided for all the pickets.

> DR. GANNON (O.S.)
> We have other ways of feeding you, Miss Paul.

DOCTOR GANNON (40s) steps from behind Alice. He grins menacingly at her.

> DR. GANNON (CONT'D)
> It's your choice.
> (extends hand)
> Doctor Gannon, at the president's service.

She can tell from his scary grin that this man is not her friend, and shakes her head at his hand.

> ALICE
> I apologize, Doctor Gannon, but I make it a habit to not shake hands with those who intend to hurt me.

He nods and circles her like a hungry predator about to attack its prey.

> DR. GANNON
> Wise habit. But... have you noticed how things have only gotten increasingly worse since the pickets started?
> (she doesn't reply)
> That is no coincidence.

                    DR. GANNON (CONT'D)
Because your friends were relaying messages for you, they
will no longer be able to receive visits or mail during the
entirety of your stay.
                        (whispers)
And it's only going to get worse. For all of you.

He grins and turns to the nurse.

                    DR. GANNON (CONT'D)
Since Miss Paul is refusing to eat, please get the guards to
come in here and help me force feed her.

INT. DISTRICT JAIL - WARD - DAY

Alice resists five guards who force her into a chair and hold her
and her head down. Doctor Gannon sadistically smirks as he
shoves a tube up her nose. Blood begins to run down the tube.

Dr. Gannon continues to push the tube up her nose until it goes
down her throat and into her stomach. A mixture of milk and raw
eggs is poured into a funnel that goes through the tube and into
her belly.

Dr. Gannon gazes into her pain-filled eyes with pleasure. When
there isn't anymore of the mixture to feed her, he violently yanks
the tube out of her nose. Alice screams. Blood *POURS* out of her
nose.
                    DR. GANNON
Sorry. We have to yank it out. If we pull too slowly, you
might vomit up what we just fed you.

The guards escort her to her new medical cell. Dr. Gannon
follows.
                    DR. GANNON (CONT'D)
There are worse places than this, Miss Paul.

MONTAGE - FORCE FEEDING ALICE

— — Alice fights the guards as they pin her to the chair to force feed her.

— — Again, she resists the daily struggle of guards pinning her down and force feeding her.

— — On one of the occasions of force feeding, the tube Dr. Gannon is pushing up her nose comes out of her mouth. Alice bites down on it like a rabid animal. She's a fighter through and through. They pull on the tube. Nothing. A guard punches her and knocks her out.

END MONTAGE

INT. WHITE HOUSE - DAY

The president is staring out the window watching the police arrest some pickets. Wilson's private secretary JOSEPH TUMULTY enters the room.

TUMULTY

The reports have come in about the conditions at the jail.

Wilson spins around to face him.

PRESIDENT

And?

TUMULTY

Some staff there even say inhumane treatment is being done to the pickets, specifically.

Wilson shoots a gust of air out of his mouth.

PRESIDENT

I need you to tell the district commissioners how very important I deem it to see there is no sufficient foundation for these statements.

Tumulty is writing this down until he realizes the president is calling for an official whitewash of inhumane treatment. He stops writing. His head rises, the whites of his eyes can be seen as he stares at the president.

                    TUMULTY
Mr. President, there are reports that Miss Paul is on the verge of death.

                    PRESIDENT
Preposterous. She is being forced to eat. I think she's gone mad. Have a psychiatrist provide a psychological evaluation on her.

Tumulty's jaw muscles flex as he writes that down, too.

                    TUMULTY
Yes, sir.

Tumulty exits. The president returns to glaring out the window.

INT. DISTRICT JAIL - WARD - DAY

Alice stares out of the broken window in her cell. She watches a bird peck at the ground, see her, and fly away. Now she's alone.

On a wall in her cell, it says, "NWP WAS HERE." Beside that in different handwriting, it says, "And where was NAWSA???" Alice touches the NWP note.

                    ALICE
And who are you that wrote this? What's your story?

She touches the other bit of writing, trying to feel connected to someone or something. The loneliness is crushingly devastating. And it drags on and on endlessly.

A knock falls on her door. She sits on her bunk. It's DOCTOR WILLIAM WHITE.

                        DR. WHITE
Hello, Miss Paul, my name is Doctor William White from Saint Elizabeth's hospital.

                        ALICE
The government-run insane asylum?

                        DR. WHITE
Yes, it is. Is that a problem for you?

When Dr. White speaks, it's with a very calm and soothing voice.

                        ALICE
Well, I am here for picketing the White House with many other women, so I am curious about what new game this is?
                        DR. WHITE
I am here to see if you need to be transferred to Saint Elizabeth's.

Alice nods.

INT. DISTRICT JAIL - LUCY'S CELL - DAY

Lucy is lying down reading a newspaper when her cell door opens. Greta enters. Lucy rises and gives her a hug. The door closes.

                        GRETA
How're you holding up?

They part.
                        LUCY
We're all on hunger strikes.

                    GRETA
Yes, we know. We're doing all we can. I'm worried about
Alice.
                    LUCY
Such a frail thing, she is.

Greta shakes her head and begins to put her property away to get
settled in.
                    GRETA
I just don't get it.

                    LUCY
Get what?
                    GRETA
How she's come to have such fortitude.

Lucy smiles at Greta and eyes her like she knows she's about to
shock her.
                    LUCY
You know, I knew her before she was as passionate as she
is now about woman suffrage.

Greta stops putting away her property and eyes Lucy. Lucy nods.

                 LUCY (CONT'D)
Yep. She was focused on her studies in England.
                 (British accent)
Just a very prim and proper lady.
                 (normal voice)
It wasn't until she was invited to "storm Parliament" that
the flames of rebellion ignited her.

EXT. PARLIAMENT - FLASHBACK - DAY

Alice, Lucy, and fifty thousand women attempt to force their way
into Parliament. Alice and many others are beaten by police. The
first strike by an officer shakes up Alice.

> LUCY (V.O.)
> That was the moment she received her first real taste of oppression. Women wanted to be heard by Prime Minister Asquith, but they were voiceless.

Alice is beaten some more and knocked down and kicked and bloodied.

INT. LONDON PRISON - FLASHBACK - DAY

Alice is beaten by guards, stripped naked, and thrown into a dirty cell with nothing in it.

> LUCY (V.O.)
> It was in hell where Alice found herself, her purpose, her passion, her reason for living.

EXT. LONDON PRISON - FLASHBACK - DAY

Alice, Lucy, and two other women exit the prison. They're bruised, have knots on their heads, and they're incredibly skinny. But Alice now has a fierceness in her eyes that wasn't there at Parliament.

> LUCY (V.O.)
> It was through all that suffering, all that pain, that bled the heroine we have today.

INT. DISTRICT JAIL - LUCY'S CELL - DAY

Greta gazes into Lucy's eyes, caught up in Alice's origin story.

> GRETA
> What doesn't kill you only makes you stronger.

Lucy smiles.

> LUCY
> If the government only knew what they were creating.

INT. DISTRICT JAIL – WARD – DAY

Dr. White exits Alice's cell grinning. Dr. Gannon is waiting for him.

DR. WHITE

I wish you luck, Miss Paul.

ALICE

Thank you.

Guard #1 locks the door after he leaves the room.

DR. GANNON

What do you think?

They walk away from Alice's cell.

DR. WHITE

I find her quite sane.
(chuckles)
She has an unusually gifted personality.

Dr. Gannon's friendly demeanor becomes tainted with disappointment.

DR. GANNON

You were sent here by the district commissioner, were you not? Who was directed by the president himself because he wanted this woman evaluated.

Dr. White stops walking, narrows his eyes at Dr. Gannon, and seems to be evaluating him.

DR. WHITE

And an evaluation is what she received.

DR. GANNON

I was under the impression the president of the United States wanted her transferred to your mental institution.

DR. WHITE

Well, I refuse to transfer her to Saint Elizabeth's.

Dr. Gannon smiles.

DR. GANNON

You'll have to excuse me, then. I have other duties to attend to. I trust you know your way out?

Without waiting for an answer, Dr. Gannon leaves Dr. White standing there staring after him.

INT. DISTRICT JAIL - WARD - DAY

Alice is looking out the window again. Dudley is approaching the warden's residence.

ALICE

Dudley!

Dudley stops, spots Alice, and rushes over to the window.

DUDLEY

I was just about to threaten the warden with a writ of habeas corpus for your treatment. They can't refuse you legal counsel, but that's exactly what they've been doing.

ALICE

Listen, they are trying to get me sent to Saint Elizabeth's. Please tell everybody at the NWP to do everything they can to prevent this.

Dudley blinks a bunch of times, processing what she has said. He shakes his head.

                         DUDLEY
I cannot believe he would stoop this low. It's criminal...
                    (snaps out of it)
I have not stopped fighting for you all, Alice. You should
know Lucy and twenty-one other women are on hunger
strikes in there with you. Everybody knows they're force
feeding you, too. Letters from men and women across the
United States are flooding the White House about the
treatment you are all undergoing. *All* know this is the
president's doing.

Alice reaches her hand out and grabs his.

                          ALICE
It's because you had the courage to step forward and
expose him.

Dudley grins.
                         DUDLEY
You may not know this, but you have staff members in
there giving the NWP daily updates on your status.

                          ALICE
                      (incredulous)
Everybody in here seems so terrible.

                       GUARD (O.S)
Hey! Get away from there!

Dudley turns and talks with the guard. The officer points at the
warden's residence. Dudley waves at Alice before heading back to
the warden's place. Alice lies down on her bed. The nurse walks
by and stops at the door.

                          NURSE
How are you, Miss Paul? Need anything?

ALICE

No, thank you.

The nurse nods and moves on. She stares at the door like the nurse is still there. Recognition comes on her: the nurse is responsible for giving the NWP updates on her status. Alice races to her cell door before she leaves.

ALICE (CONT'D)

Excuse me!
(nurse stops)
Thank you... for everything.

The nurse smiles and places a hand over her heart. She looks around to make sure nobody will hear her.

NURSE

No, Alice, thank you.

Guard #1 enters the ward, and the nurse exits. Alice lies back down on her bed.

INT. WHITE HOUSE - DAY

The president is speaking with REPORTERS. There's a sense of urgency in their eyes, erratic movements, and voices.

REPORTER

Mr. President, what do you have to say about the complaints of injustice, discrimination, and cruel treatment toward the pickets?

PRESIDENT

All it is is an extraordinary amount of lying. There is no real harshness in their treatment. I was told their bad behavior in prison fit their punishments.

JOURNALIST
What about the investigations from multiple congressmen
that further proves the credibility of the reports we've been
hearing.

PRESIDENT
(startled)
I have yet to see these reports, so I cannot speak on them.

REPORTER
These pickets have to go to court next week, so we have
your guarantee that they will look as healthy as you claim
when we see them?

The president grabs a glass of water out of fear and downs it to
give him some time to think. He also can't help looking at the exit
out of there.

PRESIDENT
If this is all you have to ask after, I will take my leave.

He gets the hell outta there.

EXT. COURT HOUSE - DAY

Reporters, photographers, and curious pedestrians await the
arrival of the picket prisoners. Two patrol wagons show up and
walking skeletons step out of one of the patrol wagons. The
second patrol wagon has wheelchairs in for them.

The last one out is Alice. She's just as bad as everyone else, but
she's always been skinny so there's not much of a difference with
her. For every single one of these women, the crowd gasps,
murmurs, and more than one let out horror-filled noises.

Flower Hat Man's narrowed eyes become sorrowful. He gapes at
these mothers, sisters, and daughters with regret.

CROWD
Shame! Shame, Mr. President.

The women are filed into court while the crowd stomps over to the White House not far away, Flower Hat Man follows them.

EXT. WHITE HOUSE - DAY

The angry crowd, after seeing Alice and the other bony women, shake their fists at the White House. Flower Hat Man joins them.

CROWD
SHAME! SHAME! SHAME!

Reporters and journalists write on their notepads, and even a couple of them join the crowd in shaming the president.

INT. WHITE HOUSE - DAY

Two congressmen are sitting down with the president as a third watches the angry crowd grow outside the White House.

CONGRESSMAN #3
The mob outside's growing.

CONGRESSMAN #2
Come away from there. You can stare at them when we leave. They're sure to still be out there.

Congressman #3 sits with them.

CONGRESSMAN #1
Mr. President, something *must* be done. I speak on behalf of the thousands of my constituents who have petitioned me about this issue.

CONGRESSMAN #2
It's the same for all of us. All across the nation there's this outpouring of anger at women being treated harshly.

CONGRESSMAN #3
Your obsession with crushing Alice Paul will lose us the Democrat House majority.

CONGRESSMAN #2
And the presidency in the next election.

The three congressman plead with their eyes. The president appears unfazed by their pleas.

CONGRESSMAN #1
Put your pride to the side, man! Think about the party! These women have *won*! It's over. Let's do what's right before we lose everything.

CONGRESSMAN #2
Show him the photos, goddamn it!

Congressman #3 hands the president a folder with a bunch of pictures of emaciated women at the jail.

CONGRESSMAN #3
Alice Paul has already stated she's coming after the party responsible for blocking woman suffrage. She's proven she's capable of obtaining results in hurting us.

CONGRESSMAN #1
And that was when she didn't have *near* the amount of support she has now.

President Wilson flips through the photos. His hard eyes soften, then moisten.
CONGRESSMAN #2
Nobody likes to see women being abused. This is why each day you fight them we lose.

CONGRESSMAN #3
Lord, help us if one of them dies in there.

CONGRESSMAN #1
Don't say that.

The president fails to hold his composure. The pictures fall to the floor. His hands cover his face as he sobs. The congressmen stare at each other, unsure of what to do.

INT. DISTRICT JAIL - WARD – DAY

Alice is lying on her bed very still, seemingly very dead. Her eyes are open and staring at nothing. Her cell door opens and she blinks. GUARD #1 glares at her.

GUARD #1
Pack up your property. You're being released.

Without moving an inch, Alice replies.

ALICE
You sure? I was sentenced to seven months in jail and it has only been a month.

GUARD #1
Don't taunt me.

Alice slowly rises. She sees a wheelchair awaits her.

ALICE
I think you know by now that I am not afraid of you.

Guard #1 smirks as she slides in the wheelchair.

GUARD #1
Yes... And to be frank, you have shown me what true strength really is.

Alice sizes him up. He's serious. She nods and takes what she can from him. She heads out and runs immediately into Dr. Gannon. He glares at her.

                              ALICE
You lost.

She eyes him, waiting for a reply. He has nothing to say. She looks
at him indignantly before wheeling herself away.

EXT. DISTRICT JAIL - DAY

Twenty-two women are escorted out of the jail in wheelchairs.
Again, the last one out is Alice. Dudley wheels her out.

Reporters, photographers, and other civilians cheer them on. As
Alice is being led out...

                            REPORTER
I'd understand if you're too weak to speak, but is there
anything you'd like to say?

Alice gestures for Dudley to stop. The crowd gathers to listen. She
uses a lot of strength for all to hear.

                              ALICE
We are put out of jail as we were put in —— at the whim of
the government. They tried to terrorize and suppress us.
They could not, so they freed us.

                           LITTLE GIRL
YAY!

Alice slumps back into her chair. Dudley wheels her away. The
crowd whistles and applauds.

INT. NWP HEADQUARTERS - DAY

The twenty-two skinny women (literally dying, which is why they
were released) are celebrated as they enter the house. Lucy is one
of them. She lost over thirty pounds during her hunger strike.

Steaming piles of food are brought to each one of them by a nurse who checks them over. A prison door brooch is pinned to each one of their coats. Each woman pinning these on them say the same thing.

                          WOMEN
          This is your prisoner of freedom brooch.

As one suffragist pins a brooch on Alice, Alice can't help but to discuss work.

                          ALICE
          How are the funds? Did we lose any members?

The suffragist smiles.

                        SUFFRAGIST
          We lost around two hundred members, but we gained
          fifteen hundred.
                          ALICE
          And the funds?
                        SUFFRAGIST
          Since you've been gone, more than eighty-six thousand
          dollars have been donated to the NWP.

Alice is speechless for a few seconds.

                          ALICE
          That is... wonderful.

A nurse checks Alice's blood pressure. Greta wheels herself over. Alice appears regretful to see Greta in such bad shape.

                          GRETA
          Don't look at me like that!
                      (grabs Alice's hand)
          Alice, I went to work for Banks to be of service. But ever
          since I met you, you have given my life such meaning and
          purpose. So, I thank you. Thank you for making me feel
          like even little ol' me can change the world with you.

Alice squeezes her hand.

ALICE
And we have.

SUFFRAGIST
But please never go into such danger again. You are too
valuable.

Harriot approaches her nodding in agreement.

HARRIOT
I give you my affection and wholehearted admiration for
what you have done. Not only for those of us who have the
joy of being associated with you, but for all women.

SUFFRAGIST
She's saying this because Congress has announced that
they're going to vote on suffrage again due to you all and
the hunger strikes.

Alice reaches out and grabs their hands.

HARRIOT
There's so much anger directed at the government now
that I'm certain your Anthony Amendment will be passed.

SUFFRAGIST
You have done so much for us during the month you've
been away. Everything is in our favor now.

Alice smiles at them in gratitude. Then she spots Dora also in a
wheelchair, a nurse with worry lines creasing her face checks over
her. She goggles Dora and squeezes Harriot's hand.

ALICE
Please wheel me over to her.

Harriot pushes her over. Dora has bruises on her face. Alice gasps at the sight of her.

> ALICE (CONT'D)
>
> Dora.

> MEDIC
>
> She's not well.

Dora slowly turns her head to Alice.

> DORA
> (weak)
>
> Hello, dear.

> ALICE
>
> When did you go in?

Dora takes a deep breath to speak, but Harriot speaks for her due to her weakened state.

> HARRIOT
>
> Right after you. They first took her to Occoquan for a bit, then to the District jail later. As you can see, they beat her.

Alice is having trouble holding onto her strength. She's on the verge of crying.

> ALICE
> (to Harriot)
>
> She may need to go to the hospital.

> DORA
>
> Do not...
> (breaths)
> ... worry yourself.

> ALICE
>
> No. You always nagged me about my health. Now it's my turn.
> (to suffragist)
> Please take her to the hospital after she eats her food.

The suffragist nods. Alice scoops up some food with a spoon, blows on it, and feeds her. Much like Dora did for her once upon a time. She also feeds herself while waiting for Dora to chew.

ALICE (CONT'D)
Come on, honey, eat up.

Eating is a struggle for Dora. She is practically lifeless. Alice stops feeding her, an urgency in her voice.

ALICE
(to suffragist)
Take her to the hospital. Now.

The suffragist and several other women drop everything and rush Dora out of there.

INT. HOSPITAL - DAY

Alice is in a wheelchair by an unconscious Dora's bedside. A suffragist is trying to get Alice to eat. Several other women are also in the room by Dora's side. Some are praying. Lucy and Harriot are on the other side of the bed.

ALICE
Didn't I just eat?

SUFFRAGIST
That was breakfast. This is lunch.

Alice accepts the plate and eats a couple bites. Dora stirs, and Alice sets the plate aside and grabs Dora's hand. Dora's eyes open.

ALICE
Hello, lovely.

Dora smiles, as does Alice. She sees Alice's food.

                        DORA
          That better not be yours.

Alice and the women laugh and cry with happiness. She sounds
much better. She even reaches over, grabs the plate, and tries to
feed Alice. More laughter.

                    DORA (CONT'D)
          Open up, honey.

Alice is so overwhelmed with joy and relief that she's laughing as
Dora spoon-feeds her.

                    DORA (CONT'D)
          I told you not to worry about me. Now look where I'm at!
          And for no reason. I'm fine.

                       HARRIOT
          You were unconscious for three days, Dora!

                        DORA
          I was tired! Can't a woman get her beauty rest?

Laughter.
                        LUCY
          The president folded under the pressure and completely
          supports the passing of the Anthony Amendment.

                        DORA
          Now that wasn't so hard, was it? When's the House voting
          on the bill?
                        ALICE
          Next month.
                        DORA
          I'm surprised you're not wheeling around lobbying to
          congressmen.

Alice reaches out to hold Dora's hand again.

                              ALICE
Well, I love you, don't I? I have to make sure you're all
right.

Dora and Alice smile warmly at each other. There is a very
powerful bond between these two.

                              DORA
You know I'm all right. Give me a day or so and I'll be back
in the fight.

Harriot claps her hands smartly. She's choking up, yet fired up.

                            HARRIOT
FIGHTERS!
                        (suppresses sob)
The lot of ya!

All are touched by those five impassioned words.

                              DORA
Fighters fight. You ladies must get back in it. I'm fine.

The women nod. They say their goodbyes. When only Alice is left,
Dora refuses to let go of her hand.

                         DORA (CONT'D)
You... need to finish your meal.

They smile.

INT. U.S. CAPITOL - DAY

Women pack the Capitol, waiting as congressman after
congressman vote for or against the Anthony Amendment.
Jeannette Rankin steps up to give her vote.

JEANNETTE

I'm proud to stand here in the United States Capitol to give my vote in support of the Anthony Amendment. Ladies, we're making history here today.

(cheers)

My vote is yes to woman suffrage.

Hours pass, but women are at the edge of their seats. Finally... a verdict is in. The house speaker makes the announcement.

HOUSE SPEAKER

The votes are in, and the recapitulation of the count for the woman suffrage amendment is 136 opposed, 274 in favor. Exactly the two-thirds majority required for the passing of — —

Cheers erupt from the suffragists. Whistles, applause, and shouts of joy ring out. The house speaker smiles. Lucy, Dora, Harriot, and all the other women begin singing.

WOMEN

Glory, glory, hallelujah. Glory, glory, hallelujah. Glory, glory, hallelujah.

Women are crying, even some politicians are choking up. They all exit the gallery singing.

EXT. U.S. CAPITOL - DAY

Carrie Catt throws her hands into the air to quiet the singing crowd. Anna Shaw stands firmly beside her. The women quiet for Carrie reluctantly. She doesn't possess the same respect she once did.

CARRIE

Ladies! Ladies! I'd just like to thank you all from the bottom of my heart for helping me get this amendment passed. If it weren't — —

SUFFRAGIST
— — WE ALL KNOW WHO PASSED THIS FEDERAL
AMENDMENT! IT WAS ALICE PAUL!

Cheers and whistles and whoops EXPLODE from the crowd. *ALL* are in agreement. Carrie tries to silence them, but the women find it in them to be LOUDER. Finally the crowd quiets on it's own.

GRETA
You *SUPPORTED* the president! *ONLY* the NWP sacrificed their time, their resources, and their *lives* to gain the political pressure to make this happen.

SUFFRAGIST
YOU have Alice to thank!

The legendary Alice Paul steps out of the crowd and slides herself between Carrie and Anna. Both of their faces show they don't like being so close to their sworn enemy.

Everybody quiets COMPLETELY for her, just like they once did for Carrie years ago.

ALICE
The NWP wouldn't be what it is today if it weren't for the NAWSA, for Carrie Catt, for Anna Shaw. We *all* played a part in this historic moment. Now let's celebrate *each other*, for the first step toward freedom has arrived.

People applaud. The icy stare Carrie and Anna had for Alice melts. All begin to sing again.

SUPER: "ONLY AFTER REPUBLICANS WON THE MAJORITIES IN BOTH HOUSES WAS ALICE'S ANTHONY AMENDMENT PASSED AND OFFICIALLY RATIFIED ON AUGUST 18, 1920."

INT. LUCY'S HOUSE - DAY

Lucy, her husband, and newborn baby sit in the living room. Lucy sings to her. She no longer resembles the badass suffragist she once was.

SUPER: "LUCY WENT ON TO GET MARRIED, HAVE KIDS, AND LIVE A LONG LIFE."

INT. DORA'S HOUSE – DAY

Dora is at home with her loving and understanding husband who's giving her a foot massage.

SUPER: "DORA FINALLY CAME HOME TO HER HUSBAND TO LIVE OUT THE REST OF THEIR DAYS AS THE ELDERLY HOMEBODIES THEY ALWAYS WERE."

EXT. LAW FIRM - DAY

Greta Graham walks into a building that has a sign above the entrance that reads, "Law Offices of Graham, Smith, and Lockheed."

SUPER: "GRETA GRAHAM WENT ON TO START A LAW FIRM THAT SPECIALIZED IN CIVIL RIGHTS VIOLATIONS. ALICE USED HER SERVICES OFTEN."

INT. NWP HEADQUARTERS - DAY

Alice is writing away like she always did. Newspapers sit besides her. Only now there isn't a buzz of suffragists working around her. She's all alone in a room.

SUPER: "ALICE WENT ON TO WRITE THE EQUAL RIGHTS AMENDMENT, HAD A CLAUSE INCLUDED AGAINST SEX DISCRIMINATION IN TITLE VII OF THE CIVIL RIGHTS ACT OF 1964, HELPED GAIN PROVISIONS FOR THE EQUAL RIGHTS OF WOMEN IN BOTH THE UNITED NATION'S

CHARTER AND THE 1948 UNIVERSAL DECLARATION OF HUMAN RIGHTS, AND MUCH MORE."

SUPER: "SHE LIVED A LONG LIFE AND DIED AT THE AGE OF 92."

FADE TO BLACK.

THE END

Author's Note

I've had a crush on Alice Paul since I first saw a documentary on the fight for women's right to vote (or something of that nature) on PBS. That was around 2019, I believe. From that point on, I wanted to read everything on Alice Paul. When you read the story on my life in the fourth installment of the Badger Book Series, you'll understand why I love her so much, though she's long dead.

Occasionally I'll find a story that I want to structure a piece around. Can anybody guess what movie structure *Pain Bleeds a Heroine's* was stolen from? Go ahead. I'll wait. . . *The Matrix*! *lol* Told you you'd never guess. = P Think about it. In the beginning of *The Matrix* there's Neo. After he's captured and released by agents, Morpheus tells him, "If they knew what I knew, you'd probably be dead." He also says Neo is "the one." There's mystery around Neo. We also know he's special. This is the same kind of beginning I tried to create with Alice Paul. We know she's perceived as some kind of threat, possesses some kind of mysterious power. But what?

I would've *loved* to recreate the same kind of impactful ending as *The Matrix*, but Alice Paul's superpower was her ability to care more about a cause than even her own life, and starvation is a weapon that takes longer than the 60-second scene Neo had.

My favorite scene to write in PBAH was after she exits the hospital, is attacked, and Alice and Lucy are *hungry* for a fight. They were ready to get back out into their battlefield. They didn't give a fuck about being battered. They were *fearless*. Really, they were warriors for a righteous cause. It's the only scene I wanted Alice to laugh in, to show how *the fight* was where she found her joy.

You really have to have the kind of passion I'm showing now about whatever you're working on in writing. Because you're going to have to spend an abundance of time reading and rereading your work, you have to believe in it. Alice Paul is somebody I could admire and believe in, though.

I should also note that I had to wing Dora and Lucy's endings. I couldn't find shit on what happened in detail regarding their lives after the right to vote was won. But I knew I had to put something. A lot of movies on real-life characters are partly fictional, though. That's why they say at the beginning of movies, "Based on a true story." Based. It can be loosely based or fully based in reality. But it's never 100 % accurate. Take the character Greta Graham, for example. She's a fictional character, but she's actually a combination of real-life characters, so she's real enough.

For those of you who haven't read the author's note in the first installment of the Badger Book Series or read my bio on my website (joshualeechaffin.com), I'm very interested in American history and reading biographies on presidents. The Woodrow Wilson biography, though? Whoo! I had that book literally collecting dust in my cell for two years. In *Would Jesus Do*

Time? I preached for us to stop judging one another, but I couldn't help myself when it came to our 28th president, especially after reading all I had on his part in Alice Paul's suffering.

He played a part in suppressing Alice Paul's consequential influence in bringing about woman suffrage, too. Paul contributed as well by shunning the spotlight. If she had granted interviews after winning the vote, wrote a book on her story, or assisted biographers in telling this amazing epic, "Alice Paul" might actually be more of a household name like Martin Luther King's and Abraham Lincoln's. I've tried to give her this name through *Pain Bleeds a Heroine.* I pray that I'm successful in this endeavor, because she deserves it.

The next bit of Badger Brew in this series is *not* political. YAY! Thank God, right? *lol* This is the only piece in the Badger Book Series that isn't political, so soak it up.

Medicaria is an original TV pilot, and it's undoubtedly the best bit of storytelling I've ever created. I'm very insecure about it, though, mainly because of its genre. It's crime, subgenre is noir. I can't help *knowing* I'll be judged because of it. The piece was spawned from an idea I had: Everybody has the capacity to kill. They merely need to be catapulted in the right situation under the perfect structural circumstances.

Without giving too much away, I wanted to take the least likely person to kill, like a doctor. I chose a paramedic since they have to deal with more crazy shit on the streets. But I took it a step further. What would it take for this medic to become a sicaria? Medic + sicaria = *Medicaria.*

Medicaria went on to win a semifinalist position in the Wiki Screenplay Contest in 2025, so don't just take my word for its quality. It'll never receive the same accolades *Would Jesus Do Time?, The Andrew Jackson Defense*, and *Eclipse City* (I pray) will earn, but it's up there as far as storytelling goes. The themes, structures, and originality of those three pieces load them in a much higher caliber of "art" that give critics nerd boners.

For any aspiring screenwriters out there, I highly recommend you armor yourselves in layers upon layers of knowledge in the craft before charging into battle with contest judges. If I didn't know what I knew when I first started writing, I would've probably quit. You'll find some great judges, but there are a good deal of judges who've left me dumbfounded as to how they stumbled on such a position.

The worst ones some might call traditionalists. I call them purists. A good indicator you're dealing with a purist is if they don't like *any* stylistic writing in narrative description blocks, they want characters' names to be in all caps all the time, and they'll even go ham on you for scene headings like "FROM THE BLACK," "FADE IN," and "BADGER'S CELL." If you obtain feedback from anybody who isn't paying attention to the actual story, I'm sorry, but you've got yourself a terrible judge. It happens, though.

If these purist judges ever read a contemporary screenplay, they'd know their "mastery" of storytelling is antiquated. Their idea of a "great" screenplays makes a script less art, less entertainment, and more cliché.

I've had scripts land in the quarterfinals, semifinals, and even win in contests, and *the exact same script* will get in the hands of some purist, and the judge will score it so low that it doesn't even make it past the first round. I once wrote a screenplay that was partly written in first-person narrative. Why? Because part of it was my story. It felt weird writing about myself in the third person. Well, I knew it should be okay to write this way since I read the *Green Book* script (a Golden Globe- and Academy Award-winning screenplay). It was partially written in first person for the same reasons as mine.

Most judges appreciated reading something different, but check out what this one purist said: "The first thing that we need to talk about is your writing style, because screenplays are never written in the first person. Novels can be written this way, and pieces of dialogue (like from a Narrator [a la FIGHT CLUB]) can be written as such, but action description is always (repeat: ALWAYS) in third person. As someone who has been analyzing materials for Hollywood decision makers for over a decade, this sort of writing was extremely jarring to me. It supremely slowed down my ability to make it through this script and understand the story. It took less than five pages for this style to completely derail my focus on the narrative."

The purist didn't stop there. *lol* There was another paragraph just as long about the exact same subject. Don't worry, I'll spare you. =) You're welcome. Here's the part that makes this judge look like a fucking idiot (forgive me, *Green Book*'s award wins also does this): This same script was entered into the biggest screenplay competition in the world—the Nicholl Fellowship. The piece was a straight banger at this place! It went through round after round, judge after judge was enamored with my work. Nobody found it "jarring." In 2021, 8,191 screenplays were entered into their contest (the most submissions they ever had up till that time), and my "work of art" knocked out over 7,000 other scripts to get into the contest's top 10 % and was just "shy" of making the quarterfinals. That's what the contest coordinator told me. How awesome is that? It might've eventually landed in the hands of a goddamn purist! Wah! *lol*

Should I pile on this judge a little more? This script she shitted on went on to receive a double recommend at another screenwriting contest. One recommend for the script, and another recommend for the writer—me! =) This was at Scriptapalooza. And this wasn't after I revised it or anything. It was the exact same screenplay. I normally enter each piece I write into at least three competitions. But to help you understand how rare a recommend is, LESS than 1 % of scripts receive a recommend in writing competitions. As you may have guessed, I received high scores in this contest, and along with the double recommend, one would think that a script in the top 1 percentile would've made it to the quarterfinals, right? Didn't happen. Why? I never found out, but one could surmise. The piece did make it to the quarterfinals in another competition, though.

I must confess, I never wrote another piece in first person again. Mainly because I didn't want to risk it getting in the hands of a purist. And there are many out there, let me tell you.

Purists undoubtedly didn't finish reading this piece due to formatting and spacing issues. They'd say it's "distracting." Amazon's programming wouldn't accept a screenplay's format. I hope it was okay for everybody else. I don't claim to be a phenomenal writer. I know I can't help myself with exposition, being preachy, and I *know* the NAWSA Convention scene is long, but I envisioned how it could *feel* like different scenes. Like when Dora pulls Alice to meet Anna, Harriot escorts her away from earhustlers, and Lucy is introduced, I imagined these *feeling* like different scenes.

Yeah, I know I'm not the best. This little prisoner is good enough to beat other writers who're better than me in contests, though! =) I believe that stems from my thorough study of Golden Globe- and Academy Award-winning screenplays. That, and reading as many books on the craft as I possibly can.

Hope you don't mind, but I have something weighing on my heart I'd like to voice, and because I can't use Facebook, Instagram, or any of those other platforms, I'd like to use this author's note to do so.

The other day I read about how Governor Sarah Huckabee-Sanders of Arkansas was kicked out of a restaurant in her own state for simply being a Republican. That should unnerve everybody, whether you're a Democrat or Republican. Her actions didn't get her kicked out, by all accounts she behaved like a model customer.

Whatever negative thing Governor Sanders may've done in the past that got her kicked out, I've done worse. All of it makes me wonder if I (a convicted murderer) would also not be welcomed to dine in restaurants if I were ever released. I suppose the Democratic South hasn't changed much? They used to do the same thing to people of color. Now they're doing it over thought crimes? The Democrat party hasn't become a fascist regime, has it? Fascism is all about intolerance, and you don't get more intolerant than enforcing thought crimes! That's pretty gross.

I'm an Independent, so I find all this political division ridiculous. I believe Barack Obama was on to something when he suggested we do away with political parties altogether, or something to that effect. That way, it would be *policies* that'd be judged, not the individuals or their parties. Let policies either stand or fall on their strengths and weaknesses. That's how it should be done.

As a student of history, I look back on how political parties change all the freaking time. The Federalists were first people who were for the newly-made Constitution. Then they became a party that was for a strong executive branch, being allied with England more than France, and liked aristocracy. The Republicans were for a stronger representative government. Later, the Republicans became Democrats, who were for slavery, and then another Republican party was formed to be an antagonistic party toward slavery. After that, the pendulum swung between them a few times.

My point is, political parties nowadays are meaningless, divisive tools with the aim to divide and conquer, in my opinion. Really, Thomas Jefferson and James Madison created the current Democrat party because there needed to be opposition to the venerated George Washington. He was such a celebrated figure, and there had to be opposition and debate over everything he did, especially as the test subject he was for a fragile republic in its infancy.

I'm curious to know if the owner, employees, and customers who didn't want Sanders in there thought that their aggressive actions would change hearts and minds in a positive way. From my experience with being in prison, love is the powerful force that changes people for the better. Hateful actions only make people dig in their heels. The hate is proof to them that they're in the right. They say, "Look at all that ugly negativity they possess! I *never* want to be like that."

Take me, for example. I'm sticking up for a Republican when I'm very aware most want me in prison for the rest of my life. Some would even go so far as to say they hate people like me. Now, I could lash out and say they're paranoid and that more consideration should be placed on human life, or I can slide my feet into their shoes. Why would anybody want to let out a murderer? There's too much risk in letting out a convicted killer, even if he's done an abundance of good and reformed himself. If he got out and killed somebody else, that would've been one murder that could've been prevented if he simply stayed in prison.

I can understand a perspective like that. Can't you? People are so busy arguing with each other that nobody's listening. I see political parties as theatrical dresses politicians wear to perform the role of their faction. Love is the only beauty that can defeat the nastiness coming out of both parties.

On love is a good way to end this, I think. Thank you all for reading my work. I'm eternally grateful for the time you took to do so. Take care and God bless.

J. L. Chaffin

April 5th, 2026